"What a great book! Andrew and Ra[...] two autistic children opened the door t[...] deeply. They learned, or should I say experienced, that the gospel isn't something you just believe; it is something you inhabit when God permits long-term suffering in your life. I'd recommend this book even if your family doesn't have a child affected by disability—it is soul food."

Paul E. Miller, Executive Director, seeJesus; author, *A Praying Life* and *A Loving Life*

"Weeping, worshiping, waiting, witnessing, and breathing. These are the constant rhythms of my life as a parent to a son with autism. These are also the rhythms of Andrew and Rachel Wilson's life, beautifully and delicately illustrated in *The Life We Never Expected*. The Wilsons have managed to do what no other authors have—provide me with clear, promising hope as a special-needs parent and allow me the sacred practice of saying, 'Me, too.' Profoundly moving and deeply rooted in the love of Jesus, this book is exactly what I needed. It is a tremendous gift."

Nish Weiseth, speaker; author, *Speak: How Your Story Can Change the World*

"This is a poignant and delightfully forthright book, written by parents who are still clearly raw from their experiences. Here is hard-earned wisdom, biblical realism, and winning sensitivity. Recommended for all in the throes of suffering and for all who would comfort them."

Michael Reeves, President and Professor of Theology, Union School of Theology, Oxford, England; author, *Delighting in the Trinity*, *The Unquenchable Flame*, and *Rejoicing in Christ*.

"Andrew and Rachel Wilson help us see how uniquely difficult it is to parent children with special needs. Their candidness is infectious, inviting us to do what the church should do: laugh with those who laugh and mourn with those who mourn. Parents of special-needs children will find compassionate solidarity, honest wrestling, voiced frustrations, and, most importantly, the gospel. Many will read this book and feel understood. Others of us need to read this book to understand, so that we can walk alongside those in the midst of hardship with compassion."

Nate Pyle, Pastor, Christ's Community Church, Fishers, Indiana; author, *Man Enough: How Jesus Redefines Manhood*

"In a striking display of honesty and depth, Andrew and Rachel Wilson explore the tension of faith and reality in this moving book. What I love most is that it's written in 'real time.' They reflect on the pain and joy not after the fact but while they are experiencing it. *The Life We Never Expected* is one of those books you have to force yourself to put down. You will laugh, you will cry, and you will celebrate the goodness of God—even in the midst of suffering."

Preston Sprinkle, Vice President of Boise Extension, Eternity Bible College; author, *People to Be Loved: Why Homosexuality Is Not Just an Issue*

"I am not a parent of children with special needs. In fact, I'm not a parent at all. Even so, I couldn't put this book down. *The Life We Never Expected* is about so much more than parenting. It is about loss, lament, hope, humility, contentment, joy—and about finding God to be more than sufficient through it all."

Karen Swallow Prior, Professor of English, Liberty University; author, *Booked: Literature in the Soul of Me* and *Fierce Convictions: The Extraordinary Life of Hannah More—Poet, Reformer, Abolitionist*

"This is a sweet and touching book—a testimony of parents' love for their special, vulnerable children, and an extended meditation on the nature of the suffering that is part of the Christian life. Andrew and Rachel write with frank honesty and a sensitivity to biblical teaching about the expectations for life in a fallen world. I hope this little book will bring wise comfort to other parents facing similar challenges."

Carl R. Trueman, Paul Woolley Professor of Church History, Westminster Theological Seminary; author, *The Creedal Imperative* and *Luther on the Christian Life*

"This is a helpful book both for those experiencing disability in their families and for those who love such families—not because of how the Wilsons are 'dealing' with disability but in how they rightly orient to our great and purposeful God. Having parented a child with multiple disabilities for more than two decades, I smiled regularly at their honest portrayal of life with disability. Anger, disappointment, and confusion along with delight and insight are offered in right measures. As both Andrew and Rachel point out, families like ours frequently do not experience the 'great resolution' about the circumstances of our lives, but we can always trust the promises of the One who made and sustains us and who will ultimately make all things new."

John Knight, Director of Donor Partnerships, desiringGod.org

The Life
We Never
Expected

Hopeful Reflections on the Challenges of
Parenting Children with Special Needs

Andrew and Rachel Wilson

Foreword by Russell D. Moore

WHEATON, ILLINOIS

Library of Congress Cataloging-in-Publication Data

Names: Wilson, Andrew, 1978–
Title: The life we never expected : hopeful reflections on the challenges of parenting children with special needs / Andrew and Rachel Wilson ; foreword by Russell Moore.
Description: Wheaton : Crossway, 2016. I Includes bibliographical references and index.
Identifiers: LCCN 2015023864 (print) I LCCN 2016009296 (ebook) I ISBN 9781433550997 (tp) I ISBN 9781433551000 (pdf) I ISBN 9781433551017 (mobi) I ISBN 9781433551024 (epub)
Subjects: LCSH: Parenting—Religious aspects—Christianity. I Child rearing—Religious aspects—Christianity. I Parents of children with disabilities. I Autism in children—Religious aspects—Christianity.
Classification: LCC BV4596.P35 W55 2016 (print) I LCC BV4596.P35 (ebook) I DDC 248.8/61989285882—dc23
LC record available at http://lccn.loc.gov/2015023864

For Pete Cooley,
a gift to the Wilsons, and to the church

Contents

Third Cycle

Fourth Cycle

Fifth Cycle

Foreword

Russell D. Moore

One of the most heroic men I ever knew was a member of a church I once served as minister. He had married very young, to a woman much older than he was. She had a son in his teenage years, and this man, not much out of his teenage years himself, was suddenly adjusting not only to marriage but to fatherhood to a developmentally disabled son. He told me that his wife, a sweet and patient woman, had been abandoned by the boy's father after he learned that his child was mentally disabled. The abandoning husband and father was an evangelical pastor. I winced at the scandal of this sorry ex-father, but I saw in the new father a picture of gospel courage and servant leadership.

This man reminded me of Joseph, who in taking Mary and our Lord as his own, faced the collapse of all his expectations for himself—and brought on himself the hostility of King Herod and the devilish tyrant behind the tyrant. He reminded me of James's admonition that pure religion is the kind that cares for widows and orphans in their distress (James 1:27). The man in my church never claimed that sort of hero status for himself. In his mind, he just did what a man does. He loved his wife, loved his family, and did what it took to make it all work. He never called it heroic. But he also never called it easy.

Maybe you or someone you love has children with disabilities or special needs. Maybe you know the joy of loving a child who pictures Christ in ways the unbelieving world could never understand. But maybe you also know just how hard it is. Maybe you know that you are sometimes, maybe often, exhausted and depleted, with your nerves wrecked and your mind confused. Maybe sometimes you wonder if it's worth it or if you have what it takes. That's what this book is about.

Andrew and Rachel Wilson write about the fact that they didn't set out to be the parents of two children with autism. They didn't picture this on their wedding day. But God had something unexpected for them—as he has something unexpected for all of us, in some way or another. This book is honest. It doesn't flinch from telling the whole truth about the trials of parenting special-needs children. Andrew and Rachel don't present themselves as experts who have tracked out every bit of the terrain in order to tell you how easy it can be if you will just do it their way. No, this is a book by gospel people. They know that they need more than what they can perform or pull together. They need grace, every day, and they need power, every day. So do I.

But as honest as this book is about the hardships, it is brimming with hope and laughter. Andrew and Rachel need to know Jesus is with them, and indeed he is. This book doesn't tell you to try harder or to be more heroic. The book shows you how to come to Jesus, just as you are, for everything you need. That's good news.

Introduction

This is a book about surviving, and thriving, spiritually when something goes horribly wrong. In our case, that "something" was discovering that both of our children had regressive autism. This book, then, is a mixture of our story and God's story, and the way in which his shapes ours.

For good reasons, we have to start a book like this with a few disclaimers. This is just our story (and it might not be yours). We're new at this (we may look back in ten years and recant it all). Our experience of special needs is mainly limited to our children (and our highs and lows may be a drop in the ocean compared to what you are facing). We don't know how to cope when children become aware of their disability (because ours haven't yet) or how to balance the needs of special-needs children and their siblings (because both of ours are autistic). And so on.

So why, you might wonder, would two novices like us write a book like this? In short, the answer is that four years ago we were looking for something like this. We were looking for a book that was not just theology or autobiography but also something that talked about spiritual survival: how, in the early tumultuous years of coming to terms with special needs, we could cling to

Jesus and even thrive in the midst of adversity. We couldn't find one, so we wrote one.

We've written with three types of people in mind. The first, obviously, is parents who have just been thrown a curveball—disability, for instance—and need encouragement to grip the Rock a little bit tighter (and to know God's grip upon them), even as the waves of life crash around them. Support groups are great. Friends who are going through the same things are invaluable. But we know that for us, nothing short of a Savior has been enough. We hope that as you read this, you will be encouraged and have your gaze continually redirected to him.

Second, we have written it for the family and friends of those who are raising children with special needs. We can't claim to know what it's like for everyone else, but we suspect some of our experiences will be shared by others—so if you're trying to come to terms with what's happening to people you love, this may be useful.

And third, we've written it for a broader audience, including anyone who is suffering at the moment and wants to know how to lament, worship, pray, wait, and hope. Our story may well be very different from yours, but the odds are that the ways God calls us to respond are fairly similar. So our prayer is that, whoever you are, this book will help you find God and lean on him in the storm.

We should also say, we took a deliberate decision to write while things are still raw for us, and that rawness (and inexperience) will probably come through these pages. Who knows? Maybe in twenty years' time, we'll be able to write a book about how God's purposes have been carefully woven through the fabric of our lives—and our family. But for now, we are feeling for them in the dark. Perhaps you are too.

The list of people who have helped us while we've been writing this volume—family, friends, educational and medical professionals, caregivers, social workers, church members, prayers, encouragers—is so long that it would take a whole book just to name them all. But there are a few people whom we just have to thank publicly. Our parents have been astonishingly supportive, helpful, generous, encouraging, flexible, creative, and sacrificial, and they have rescued us from many disasters, either by showing up to help or by taking the children so we could have a bit of space—and sleep. Our friends and fellow leaders at Kings Church, Graham and Belinda Marsh and Steve and Ann Blaber, not only encouraged us in the writing of this book but read through and commented on the manuscript toward the end of the process, which made the book much better than it would otherwise have been. We also received invaluable feedback from Debra Reid, Charles and Nikki Glass, and our excellent editor for the original edition published in the UK, Eleanor Trotter (at Inter-Varsity Press, Nottingham, England). Our friends Stephen and Emma Dawson found time in their busy lives to help us with the Q&A section, and for this, we are really grateful. And then there is the incomparable Pete Cooley, who has lived with us for two years and endured more early starts, shouts, glares, scratches, interrupted nights, meltdowns, and hissy fits than anyone should have to (and that's just from Andrew). For them, and for the many others whose support has made life workable over the past few years, we will always be thankful.

Andrew and Rachel Wilson

February 2015

The Day of Deep Breaths

Rachel

Some days require a lot of deep breaths. That's true for every parent, but my guess is that it's intensified when you have children with special needs. For me, Thursday, August 4, 2013, was one of those days. Remembering it, even months later, brings on a weird combination of shudders, tears, and giggles.

We're on vacation, but it's an early start anyway. Zeke wakes at 4:30 a.m., and Andrew starts the day with him. (Vacations with our children are usually more exhausting than normal life, partly because the kids have their sleep routines messed up by being in a new place—in this case, a house belonging to friends who are away on vacation—and partly because the normal support, from school, nursery, parents, and friends, isn't there.) After an hour or so, Anna is up, the first DVD of the day is nearly finished, and breakfast is about to get started: Cheerios with milk for Anna, dry Weetabix (yes, I know) for Zeke. So far, so good.

Then Andrew wakes me up to tell me he's just vomited.

This happens sometimes, obviously. Men get sick. I suspect men who have been tired for two years get sick more often than most, and those surrounded by the kind of antics I'm about to describe get sick more often still. But this is now round three of the second sick bug of the summer holidays—as in, Anna, then Zeke, then a two-week break when nobody is sick, then Anna, then Zeke, and now Andrew—and I'm beginning to find it annoying. I stare at him in dismay, hoping he's joking. He isn't.

I take a deep breath, get up, and go downstairs.

My appearance somehow makes it a matter of intense urgency that the *Oliver and Company* DVD case be found and handed to Zeke. We've now gotten used to the randomness of Zeke's obsessions, but it can still be wearing—the *Oliver and Company* DVD case, not the DVD itself, and certainly (God forbid) not the video; the branded cover inside but removable; the location of the case in Zeke's carefully laid-out line of twenty other cases; the explosive reaction to any interference with said line, especially from his sister; the unique and often incomprehensible words that summon the case to be brought ("Hoffer and Pumpnee! Hoffer and Pumpnee!"); the bouncing up and down and hand flapping that follow its arrival; and the rest. Knowing that a *no* will cause an outburst but a *yes* will cause repetitive behaviors for several hours, and it's still only 6:15 a.m., I deny the request. Zeke repeats it. I deny it. (Bargaining at this stage is pointless.) Zeke repeats it. I deny it. Repeat eleven times. The inevitable outburst comes.

I take another deep breath.

After a few minutes of successfully engaging Zeke in a "normal" activity—sorting his cases, pulling the dog's ears, or some equivalent—it occurs to me that Anna has been in the living room for a while but that things have gone suspiciously quiet. I walk down the hall to investigate. On entering the living room, I find Anna with her face submerged in the open-lidded fish tank, happily blowing bubbles into the water, while floating fish flakes bob about on the surface and bewildered guppies swim around her cheeks in confusion. I knew that Anna loved the sensory experience of face dipping, having done it all summer with paddling pools and occasionally even sandpits, but it never occurred to me that she would do it in something so aromatically unpleasant and manifestly dirty as a fish tank. *No wonder everybody in this family gets sick so often*, I muse to myself. Another deep breath. For a moment, I wonder if it's worth grabbing a camera but decide instead to retrieve my three-year-old from the tropical waters and then set about drying the walls.

I return to the kitchen. Zeke, who had been happily rummaging through his cases, has somehow managed to slide a carving knife off the countertop and is running around the kitchen with it, whooping with delight. Another deep breath. At this point I have some difficult choices to make. Anna is dripping wet, and Zeke is at serious risk of either slicing his forearm or beheading the dog. Yet I know from experience that either shouting at him or running toward him to retrieve the knife will make him think we're playing a game and run away laughing, and that will instantly make matters much worse. So I amble nonchalantly toward him, with my body language saying, *This isn't a life-or-death thing; it's no big deal*, while my mind is racing with the thought, *This might be a life-or-death thing, and it's a very big deal*. Remarkably, it works. I retrieve the knife, put all the other knives out of reach, and head upstairs to get Anna into some dry clothes.

A few minutes later, more suspiciously quiet behavior, this time from Zeke, leads me back downstairs to the hallway, where I find the front door now wide open. I run out into the road in a panic, looking up and down the street for him, and then notice that he is sitting behind the car in the driveway playing with stones. Another deep breath. I take him back inside and double-lock the front door. The next few minutes pass without incident, and I manage to finish packing lunches, pile the kids into the car, and head off to a nearby adventure farm, where we arrive just as it opens in order to avoid Anna's greatest enemy: other people.

All things considered, the farm trip is a success. The children cope, the meltdowns are limited, and although I'm on my own with them, nobody dies. But there are still a few incidents. The jumping cushion is surrounded by the shavings of recycled car tires, which are perfect for Zeke to sit there and chew while he decides whether he feels like jumping or not. Anna, who is mid-regression at this point, marches onto it with confidence and starts bouncing, but then another child makes physical contact with her, and she withdraws into shutdown mode, refusing to make eye contact, speak, or play for the rest of the morning. We go on a beautiful tractor ride: Zeke loves it and shrieks throughout, not because of the animals but because of the enormous rotating tires, but Anna buries her face in my shoulder and notices nothing. I carry her for the next two hours and reflect on the fact that, for all the face dipping, vomiting, front-door opening, and carving-knife waving my day has involved, much the hardest part of it is to fight the tears when I think of how my little girl has gone backward in the space of a year, from a chatty little person who plays and sings to a frightened baby who has lost nearly all her vocabulary and most of her social skills. Another deep, painful breath. I change her diaper, trying to give her a little privacy behind some play equipment, and while I'm there, Zeke obstructs the slide for the many other children who have now arrived, causing frustrated parents to look around for a responsible adult. It's tempting to pretend it isn't me.

Before heading home, we enjoy a picnic lunch, and the kids are peaceful and settled. While they're eating, I phone the hospital for the third time to hunt down a pair of reinforced Piedro boots[1] for Zeke, which no hospital department seems to be taking responsibility for losing, and check my messages to see if the latest blood test results for Anna are back, which they aren't. Another deep breath. On the way home, I think about buying milk, but since I can't take the kids into a shop on my own without—well, by now you can probably imagine—I decide that tea with soy milk isn't so bad after all, and we go home without any dairy. I make sure to double-lock the front door when we get inside, check that the fish have survived their close Anna encounter earlier in the day, and then all but cover the tank with plastic wrap to make sure it doesn't happen again. I put on a DVD for the children and take one more deep breath.

One day, I say to myself, I'm going to laugh about this. I may even write a book about it.

Psalm 130

Out of the depths I cry to you, O Lord!
    O Lord, hear my voice!
Let your ears be attentive
    to the voice of my pleas for mercy!

If you, O Lord, should mark iniquities,
    O Lord, who could stand?
But with you there is forgiveness,
    that you may be feared.

I wait for the Lord, my soul waits,
    and in his word I hope;
my soul waits for the Lord
    more than watchmen for the morning,
    more than watchmen for the morning.

O Israel, hope in the Lord!
    For with the Lord there is steadfast love,
    and with him is plentiful redemption.
And he will redeem Israel
    from all his iniquities.

What Do We Do with Suffering?

A MEDITATION ON PSALM 130

Andrew

It is hard to think of a generation in history that has suffered less than mine. I'm a British millennial, and that means my life has been almost entirely free of the things that make life on planet earth awful: bloody wars, infant mortality, ethnic cleansing, tuberculosis, earthquakes, child trafficking, smallpox, the Osmonds. Yet the strange thing is, my generation struggles with the problem of suffering more, not less, than most of those who have gone before us. I have experienced far, far less pain and difficulty in my short life than almost anyone else in any period of history, yet I probably struggle with it—philosophically, emotionally, even theologically—more than the countless women who have lost babies in childbirth, lost husbands in war, and then died before they even reached my age. It's like the less we have suffered, the less equipped we are to deal with it.

That's why the Psalms are so powerful. They don't avoid the problem of pain, and they don't explain it away; they tackle it head-on, and in doing so, they help us process our distress in ways that actually fit with the realities we're experiencing. They give us the words and emotions of seasoned sufferers, and they train us how to respond honestly, wisely, and well. And one of the best examples, as well as one of the most condensed, is Psalm 130. Walk through it with me for a moment.

The psalm begins where we all are supposed to begin when tragedy strikes—with weeping:

> Out of the depths I cry to you, O LORD!
>> O Lord, hear my voice!
> Let your ears be attentive
>> to the voice of my pleas for mercy!

This is an anguished start. It's not a careful, measured reflection on the nature of pain or an attempt to explain it. (We don't even know what the problem is at this point.) It's a cry from the depths, a desperate plea for mercy, accompanied by red eyes, sniffling, tissues, shaking shoulders, and jowls smeared with saltwater.

That's where our response to suffering is meant to begin. Many of us, fueled by fears, doubts, or insecurities, want to rush in with questions ("How could God let this happen to us?"), answers ("This must be happening because of *this*"), advice ("We/ you should start doing *that*"), or plain silly comments ("It will be all right"). Others of us want to handle it by posting about it on social media, which runs the risk of confusing an instant reaction with a considered response. But there's a place for just wailing about it, like Jesus did when his friend died and like the psalmists seemed to do all the time. We need to learn—especially those of us from Western cultures where mourning is so understated—how to grieve in a way that gives due weight to what has happened to us. Otherwise, in our attempt to cope with the situation, we can trivialize the pain and so fail to deal with it properly.

Having said that, there comes a point when, after a period of weeping, the believer begins worshiping God in the darkness:

> If you, O LORD, should mark iniquities,
>> O Lord, who could stand?
> But with you there is forgiveness,
>> that you may be feared.

This line helps us see what the psalmist was crying about: he has sinned against God and needs mercy. That's why he starts reflecting on God's overwhelming grace and the ever-present offer of forgiveness. But even when our grief is of a different sort than this—prompted by sickness, death, poverty, persecution, or whatever—this is a wonderful way to respond to it. With the darkness all around us and the wounds still fresh, we lift our tear-stained faces to God and begin to worship him for the gospel.

Raising autistic kids is painful. This morning Zeke was up for the day at 3:30 a.m., Anna was grinding her teeth constantly from the moment she awoke, Zeke was shouting relentlessly about some cartoon character or other—when you haven't slept much, they all blend into one!—and Rachel and I were both on the verge of tears before the working day had even started. Some days we just look at our lives and think, *This is awful*. And sometimes it is.

Yet when I begin to worship God for the gospel, things start looking very different. Through the exhausted frustration, I remind myself, God has not "marked my iniquities." He has forgiven me for every sordid, spiteful, and shameful thing I've ever done. He has rescued me from a life in which the crying and teeth grinding continue not just for a few hours on a Thursday morning but forever in eternity. He has treated me according to his mercy, rather than my performance. He has secured for me a future of eternal and unimaginable joy, which is thoroughly out of step with what I deserve. As I consider these things, and praise my Father for them, my weeping slowly turns to worshiping, just like the psalmist's does.

With all that said, though, the pain is still there. Celebrating the gospel is beautiful and is good for my soul, but it doesn't make me sleep more or cry less. Until God fixes everything, I'm still waiting:

> I wait for the LORD, my soul waits,
> > and in his word I hope;
> my soul waits for the Lord
> > more than watchmen for the morning,
> > more than watchmen for the morning.

You can't process suffering properly unless you remember that Christianity, like Judaism, is a religion of waiting. The world is not yet fixed. One day there will be no autism and no suffering whatsoever, but until that day, we wait. That's what makes life so exasperating sometimes, especially for those of us who are naturally impatient.

It's also what makes it full of hope, though. For the believer, waiting is not wishful thinking, as if we're waiting for a train or a parcel that may or may not come. Waiting for the Lord is a waiting grounded in certainty, based on his promise ("In his word I hope"), similar to the way watchmen wait for the morning. You don't get a lot of watchmen these days, but I've got a feeling they don't sit there at 3:00 a.m. thinking, *My goodness, this night's gone on a long time. Perhaps morning has been cancelled today! Maybe the earth has stopped at this particular point in orbit, and the sun is never going to rise again.* Watchmen wait for the morning not because they think it's coming but because they know it is. The night is dark, but the light always breaks.

That's how to wait for the Lord. I take great comfort from emperor penguins on this one: there's something about the way they huddle together to protect themselves from Antarctic blizzards, each of them keeping a solitary egg above its feet through months of frozen darkness, that says, *This is almost unbearable, and it's almost worth quitting, but the sun is on its way. Hang in there, brothers. The light always breaks.* I want to wait for the return of Jesus like that. More than watchmen wait for the morning and more than penguins wait for the sunrise.

Finally, as the psalmist closes his short song, he begins witnessing, testifying about God's goodness to the people around him:

> O Israel, hope in the LORD!
>> For with the LORD there is steadfast love,
>> and with him is plentiful redemption.
> And he will redeem Israel
>> from all his iniquities.

None of us suffers alone. Even in those bleak times when nobody understands and the darkness is our only friend, there are multitudes of believers who have been there before us, and many of them still witness to us out of the shadows. "Whatever my lot, Thou hast taught me to say, 'It is well, it is well with my soul,'" said Horatio Spafford after his daughters had just died.[2] "The bud may have a bitter taste, but sweet will be the flower," wrote William Cowper, a poet who struggled daily with depression and suicidal thoughts.[3] For forty centuries or more, worshipers of Israel's God have wept, worshiped, waited, and then borne witness to a steadfast love that cannot be broken, no matter what the circumstance. Their words are a profound source of comfort and encouragement to the rest of us.

As we come to terms with our pain and see the love of God at work in spite of it and even through it, we eventually reach the point when we can add our voice to that crowd of witnesses and testify to the ways in which *we* have found God to be faithful.

That's the destination we are heading toward eventually. One of the most exciting things that ever happens in our church is when ordinary people, who have suffered hardship and carried scars for months or years, come to the microphone and witness to the goodness of God through suffering. When we cut to the last page and see all that the Father has done, we want nothing more than to tell others about it: "With the LORD there is steadfast love!"

But much of our lives, and much of yours, is not lived on the last page. Many of us are so impatient to get there that in our pain, we flunk the weeping or the waiting (or, worse, foist our impatience onto others who are suffering, adding a dollop of guilt to the distress they are already experiencing). So rather than writing about how we get there as soon as possible—and if your story is anything like ours, you'll find you're continually making progress and then going backward anyway, as if playing a giant game of Snakes and Ladders—we've structured this book in five sections (weeping, worshiping, waiting, witnessing, and breathe) to try to help people who are processing each particular stage. Our story involves a confusing mixture of sadness, singing, silence, and celebration. So did the psalmist's. And chances are that yours will too. So we've tried to be honest about the challenges of each part, as well as the opportunities.

Don't get me wrong. Everybody loves it when the sun comes out and the female penguins return and the bereaved person finds contentment and the victim finds restoration and the autistic child flourishes. That's where the whole of creation is headed, little by little, and I'm so, so grateful that it is. But there are many times in between when being a penguin stinks. Trust me.

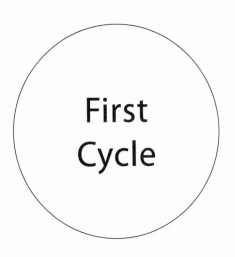

First
Cycle

The Orange

Andrew

Finding out your children have special needs is kind of like being given an orange.

You're sitting with a group of friends in a restaurant. You've just finished a decent main course and are about to consider the dessert menu when one of your friends gets up, taps his glass with a spoon, and announces that he has bought desserts for everyone as a gift. He disappears around the corner and returns a minute later with an armful of round objects about the size of tennis balls, each beautifully wrapped with a bow on top.

As he begins distributing the mysterious desserts, everyone starts to open them in excitement, and one by one, they discover that they have each been given a chocolate orange. Twenty segments of rich, smooth, lightly flavored milk chocolate—a perfect conclusion to a fine meal and a very sociable way of topping off an enjoyable evening. The table is filled with chatter, expressions of gratitude between mouthfuls, and that odd mixture of squelching sound and intermittent silence that you always get when a large group is filling their faces. Then you open your present.

You've been given an orange. Not a chocolate orange; an actual orange. Eleven segments of erratically sized, pith-covered pulp, with surprisingly large pips in annoying places, requiring a degree in engineering in order to peel it properly, the consumption of which inevitably involves having juice run down to (at least) your wrists, being squirted in the eye with painful acid, and spending the remainder of the meal picking strands the size of iron filings out from between your molars. You stare at the orange in front of you with a mixture of surprise, confusion, and disappointment. The rest of the table hasn't noticed. They're too busy enjoying their chocolate.

You pause to reflect. There's nothing wrong with oranges, you say to yourself. They are sharp, sweet, refreshing, and zesty. The undisputed kings of the citrus fruit world—when did you last order a freshly squeezed *lemon* juice?—oranges are enlivening and flavorsome, filled with vitamin C, and far better for you than the mixture of sugar, milk powder, cocoa butter, and milk fat your friends are greedily consuming. With a bit of practice, you can probably peel them without blinding your neighbors. In fact, looking at the scenario from a number of perspectives—medical, dietary, environmental—you have actually been given a better dessert than everyone else. And you didn't have a right to be given anything anyway.

But your heart sinks all the same. An orange was not what you expected; as soon as you saw everyone else opening their chocolate, you simply assumed that was what you would get too. Not only that, but it wasn't what you wanted—you could pretend that it was and do your best to appreciate it and be thankful, but you really had your heart set on those rich, smooth, lightly flavored milk-chocolate segments. And because you're surrounded by other people, you have to come to terms with the sheer unfairness of being given your orange, while your friends enjoy, share, laugh about, and celebrate theirs. A nice meal has taken an unexpected turn, and you suddenly feel isolated, disappointed, frustrated, even alone.

Discovering your kids have special needs is like that.

Before we become parents, we have all sorts of ideas, expectations, and dreams about what it will be like. These ideas come from our own childhood (whether good or bad), from the media, and from seeing the experiences of our friends and relatives: pushing strollers with sleeping babies along the riverside, teaching our children to walk, training them how to draw with crayons rather than eat them, answering cute questions, making star charts, walking them to school. We don't look forward to the more unpleasant aspects of parenting—interrupted nights, diapers, tantrums—but because we know that they will come, and because we know that they will pass, we are emotionally prepared for them. Mostly, we daydream about the good bits and talk to our friends about the joys and challenges of what we are about to take on.

Then something happens. For some of us, it is at a twelve-week scan or at birth; for others, it is several months or even years later. But something happens that tells us, somehow, that all is not well. We'll talk a bit more about this later, but for now, it's enough to say that it rocks everything, and the entire picture of our lives, both in the present and the future, gets repainted in the course of a few hours. Gradually, as time starts to heal, we come to terms with the situation, and we learn that there are some wonderful things, besides the difficult and painful things, about what we've been given. Yet we can't help feeling isolated, disappointed, frustrated, even alone.

Special needs, like the orange, are unexpected. We didn't plan for them, and we didn't anticipate them. Because our children are such a beautiful gift, we often feel guilty for even saying this, but we might as well admit that we didn't *want* our children to have autism any more than we wanted them to have Down's syndrome, cerebral palsy, or whatever else. Give or take, we wanted pretty much what our friends had: children who walked at one, talked at two, potty trained at three, asked questions at four, and went off to public school at five. We could have lived quite happily without knowing what Piedro boots were for, what stimming[4] was, or how to fill out DLA (Disability Living Allowance) forms. So there are times when we're wiping the citric acid out of our eyes and watching our friends enjoying their chocolate, when it feels spectacularly unfair, when we wish we could retreat to a place where everyone had oranges, so we wouldn't have to fight so hard against the temptation to comparison shop and wallow in self-pity. We know that oranges are juicy in their own way. We know that they're good for us and that we'll experience many things that others will miss. But we wish we had a chocolate one all the same.

In our case, that feeling has become less acute and less frequent over time. Our appreciation for the wonders of tangy citrus and vitamin C has increased, and our desire for milk fat and cocoa butter has diminished. But in our story, so far, it hasn't disappeared. I'm not sure it ever will. And that's okay.

The Call to Sacrifice

Rachel

I received an email recently which ended with the words, "You are such a rich woman."

Emails about the children don't usually say that. Normally, they are of the sympathetic, sighing type: "I don't know how you do it," or "Things must be so tough for you." So this one really caught me off guard. It gave my feelings of mild self-pity a resounding slap and made me want to let out a knee-jerk response: "Rich? I'm spent! Done! I have nothing left in my account to give."

Yet the strange thing is that as I headed into the adult Christian life, "spending myself on behalf of the needy" was my aim, my life's mission. As a teenager, I was inspired by the lives of missionaries past and present, men and women of faith like George Müller and Jackie Pullinger who made huge personal sacrifices for the sake of the poor and needy. I used to live on stories like Pullinger's *Chasing the Dragon* (1980) and Sarah De Carvalho's *The Street Children of Brazil* (1996). So considering that I have no problem with sacrifice in itself and that I went into the Christian life with my eyes open, what's the problem?

The eye-wincing truth is that I had imagined my mission field might be a brothel of trafficked women or a schoolyard of African orphans. I thought the sacrifices would be more obvious and profiled and the yield (or harvest) that came from sleepless nights or leaving loved ones behind more tangible than they are. "Yes, I left my family and home comforts behind," I could imagine telling the breathless BBC correspondent, "but curing Ebola was worth it." Somehow, raising children with special needs doesn't have quite the same ring to it.

But the Lord is my Shepherd. I really do believe that. And for some reason, my Shepherd has led me to this field rather than that one. This mission field with these two beautiful, bottomless wells who require all my energy, strength, and patience. Sometimes it seems like a wasteful use of all these resources, resources that could have been used to feed the poor. Whenever it does, I try to remember my Shepherd sitting in a house a few miles from Jerusalem:

> Now when Jesus was at Bethany in the house of Simon the leper, a woman came up to him with an alabaster flask of very expensive ointment, and she poured it on his head as he reclined at table. And when the disciples saw it, they were indignant, saying, "Why this waste? For this could have been sold for a large sum and given to the poor." But Jesus, aware of this, said to them, "Why do you trouble the woman? For she has done a beautiful thing to me." (Matt. 26:6–10)

Jesus, my Shepherd, doesn't seem to appraise value in the same way as I do. His spreadsheet is completely different from mine. He is interested in the wasteful expenditure of love and energy, just because it's in keeping with the sort of crazy love and sacrifice he showed in his life and death. His call to sacrifice is the same whether I'm standing in an African field or in a kitchen with a child who for the 365th time this year needs to be cajoled into finishing a few spoonfuls of noodles. This certainly isn't the sacrifice I would have chosen to make. But I remember standing in a meeting a few years ago and clearly saying to God, like Ruth to Naomi, "Your people shall be my people" (Ruth 1:16). Well, these two are his people, and now they're my people.

For those of us who are mothers (and fathers), God wants us to esteem the field he's given us. It's not a tiring distraction from the true mission field we should be tilling; these are *our* people, for us to reach and for us to be trained and transformed as we do. Not only that, but in our giving, as we willingly lay down our lives, he smiles on us, because as Christ explained, "Whatever you did for one of the least of these brothers and sisters of mine, you did for me" (Matt. 25:40 NIV). All the sacrifices, the diaper changing, the feeding, the dealing with meltdowns—they cannot be worth it if they're just for our children. But they're not. Ultimately, they are a perfume poured out for him.

It can be so easy, though, to look for more immediate sources of praise. Eight years ago, I did an internship program for a human rights organization in Washington DC. On the first day, the CEO welcomed us in a staff breakfast, and as part of his address, he handed us each a small trumpet key ring. He told us that there would be times when, out for drinks with interns in corporate law or accountancy, it would suddenly be tempting to belittle their sacrifices or hard work by subtly (or not so subtly) reminding them that while they work to make rich clients richer, we work long hours to free slaves. At times like these, he told us, we were to look at our trumpet key rings and make a conscious choice not to blow our own trumpets. Faced with a room of young, passionate, but competitive interns, it was a pretty perceptive welcome.

I still think about that trumpet. And there are days, even now, when it is tempting to blow my own trumpet, whether by looking for recognition in the wrong places or by belittling the parenting trials that the people around me face. In a room full of women bemoaning the fact their children won't try broccoli, it can be tempting to throw in a conversational bomb like "Yes, but does anyone have any strategies on stopping smearing?" The truth is, as a parent, you wield a certain amount of power to make people feel bad about their own challenges or to make them live in awe and admiration of yours. Being open and honest with trusted friends is great, as is receiving their encouragement and affirmation. You need it! But the life sacrifices are ultimately for an audience of One.

Parenting in a daily willingly-laying-down-your-life way is a powerful opportunity to reflect and enact what the gospel truly is. But it is just a reflection, a role play, if you will—because there is no humbling moment, no public humiliation or social isolation that matches what Jesus experienced at the cross. We have a High, Priest who fully sympathizes with all our weaknesses and gave himself up as the centerpiece of our faith. Giving up our lives for others is the centerpiece of our faithfulness.[5] The call to Christ is a call to sacrifice—to suffering, death, and burial—and through that sacrifice, to resurrection and fruitfulness. So yes, today, I am spent. But in the gospel, I am rich. My friend was right.

The True Battle

Rachel

If, in the weeks that followed Anna's diagnosis, you had taken a page out of the *News of the World*'s book and hacked our home phone, you would have had no doubt that a battle was underway.[6]

I ran around like a headless chicken. I trawled the Internet for news of funds, equipment, and services to which we might be entitled. I spent hours documenting the children's behavior and needs. I quickly got on first-name terms with several medical secretaries. I chased down professionals for the latest reports and the soonest-available appointments.

As it happens, I think that all the hard work I did was, in the end, in the children's best interests. But—and this is one of the key points of the book you're now reading—the true battle was elsewhere.

You see, as important as school places and car seats and strollers and boots are, they are peripheral. They sometimes look like the most important thing going on in a particular day, but they never are. All of them, one day, will expire, pile up in a landfill somewhere, be eaten by moths, decay, or degrade. And if I don't realize that, they will continue to distract me from where the true battle is being fought: in the two-pint, gray lump of squidge behind my face.

Of the many helpful things I have read during our journey with the children, a paragraph from Rachel Jankovic, who at the time of writing had five preschool children, rises to the top of the pile. She writes,

> If there is anything I have learned in the course of my fast and furious mothering journey, it is that there is only one thing in my entire life that must be organized. The kids can be running like a bunch of hooligans through a house that appears to be at the bottom of a toaster, and yet, if organization and order can still be found in my attitude, we are doing well. But if my attitude falters, even in the midst of external order, so does everything else.[7]

She is so right. I could have a rolling schedule of every therapy under the sun—private drumming lessons, funding for horse handling, a private school place, even a fully equipped sensory room in my house—but if my mind is not settled toward God as the author of it all, and if I am not putting him first, I might as well quit. It will all be in vain; it won't bring me any peace, and the true battle is being lost.

The reverse is true too. Zeke could be running laps and flapping his hands in one corner, Anna could be wandering in circles and grinding her teeth in another, and the floor between them could look like the results of an explosion in a children's center. But if, through it all, my thoughts are ordered, and I am able to see my circumstances in a God-shaped way, then the true battle is being won.

What is exasperating is this: I can have days in which I win several fake battles, but in doing so, I lose the true one. The fake battles are a whirlwind of phone calls, government services, websites, more phone calls, forms, applications, more phone calls. And each of these can distract me from the true battle, which, more often than not, is not fought that way. Frequently, the weapons of the true battle include silence, prayer, thought, clinging onto a recently read Scripture passage with my fingernails, singing through gritted teeth, reading a prewritten prayer out loud, reaching for Jesus through the mist of confusion or unanswered prayer, stilling myself in his presence, and remembering that he is good and faithful and kind. So distinguishing between the fake battles and the true one, between what I can do and what I must do, is critical. Phone calls and social workers can wait. Centering my thoughts on God cannot.

I love my kids most not by loving them the most but by first loving God. As soon as I take my eyes off him and my attitude falters and I begin to believe that I alone must push for them and control their destinies, the unbearable weight of playing God soon becomes apparent. When I put my eyes back on the One who always deserves my attention, then whatever fake battles are being lost around me, the true one is being won. It makes all the difference.

Individualitis and the Dung Gate

Andrew

For many years, I have suffered from individualitis. It's a debilitating yet curiously common disease of the soul, and it's especially common among young, rich, Western people. It comes in many forms, but its primary symptom is the unshakable belief that the world is mainly about *me*.

I don't know where I caught it. It could have been at boarding school, where I was taught that I should "blaze my trail," and that we were probably going to end up being masters of the universe. It could have been at university, where academics and recruiters insisted that the world was our oyster. (It isn't, of course. It's an enormous ocean, much of which is dark and unknown, and it's got plenty of oysters, as well as thousands of creatures that are just like you, and millions of creatures that want to eat you, and billions of creatures who will never know who you are.) It might have been with me from birth. It might even have come from the church; I remember singing songs about my personal destiny and how I was going to be a history maker and how although everybody else was ordinary, I was going to be different. Probably, it was a mixture—but wherever it came from, I caught it.

The really worrying thing, as I look back, was that I didn't realize it was a problem. It wasn't until much more recently that I came across a paragraph from Carl Trueman that punched this whole way of thinking on the nose:

> The belief that we are each special is, by and large, complete tosh. Most of us are mediocre, make unique contributions only in the peculiar ways we screw things up, and could easily be replaced as husband, father or employee, by somebody better suited to the task. . . . [Yet] far too many Christians have senses of destiny which verge on the messianic. . . . Put bluntly, when I read the Bible it seems to me that the church is the meaning of human history; but it is the church, a corporate body, not the distinct individuals who go to make up her membership. . . . My special destiny as a believer is to be part of the church; and it is the church that is the big player in God's wider plan, not me.[8]

The man's got a point.

But I had never seen it that way. I thought I *was* special, unique, irreplaceable. In fact, individualitis affected every area of my life. I thought individualistically about purpose ("my purpose in life" rather than "our purpose in life") and Scripture ("this passage is for me" rather than "this passage is for us"). I thought that way about the church (which serves me), the gospel (which is about rescuing me), cultural change (which happens when great individuals rise up and do something), and evangelism (which is about individual people sharing their stories). Most of all, I thought that way about *calling*: Rachel and I both had one, and it was up to each of us to find out what our own callings were and then fulfill the roles that only *we* could. It was encouraging to hear just how much of God's big plan depended on *us*.

Then our lives hit the wall. You know all about that by now. Suddenly, the future we had imagined—saving the world through preaching, writing, advocacy, intervention, and traveling around the globe—was completely reconfigured. Before we found out about the children, it was sort of imaginable that we could be fruitful for God on our own. (Sort of imaginable.) But from that point on, it became utterly *un*imaginable. These days, we can't even get through the day without the church, let alone save the world. We are totally dependent on a community of people—people who help, encourage, pray, serve, take responsibility—to be fruitful in any way at all. Without them, we're like branches without a tree, parts without a body, stones without a building. Which is just how God wants it.

One of my biblical heroes is a guy named Malchijah, who pretty much debunks individualitis on his own. You've never heard of him. Almost nobody has. He sits, marooned, in the middle of an incredibly long and dull list of names in Nehemiah 3, which is a chapter about the wall of Jerusalem being repaired. It lists all the builders, one by one: Eliashib, who built the Sheep Gate; the sons of Hassenaah, who built the Fish Gate; Hasshub, who helped repair the Tower of the Ovens; and so on. And in verse 14, buried in with all the others, is Malchijah the son of Rechab, who repaired the Dung Gate. The *Dung* Gate. I'll just let that sink in for a moment. (I imagine he would rather have been allocated the Tower of the Ovens.)

The reason why Malchijah is my hero is this: he wasn't a hero. He didn't lead Israel, kill any bad guys, or have a book named after him. We don't actually know anything else about him. All we know is that he spent a short period of his life doing something very mundane, very smelly, and very unnoticeable: he fixed a Dung Gate. Yet in his mediocre, ordinary way, Malchijah—

along with Eliashib, Hasshub, the sons of Hassenaah, and all the others—established the kingdom of God on earth.

I say that because ancient cities depended on their walls to keep them safe, and their walls were only as strong as their weakest point. So if 98 percent of the wall of Jerusalem was perfectly restored and the Dung Gate was a tumbledown mess, then an enemy could simply attack there, and the city would fall. There is no use whatsoever in building *part of* a wall or having a wall that is *mostly* secure. (Just ask the guys who built the Maginot Line.) So if Malchijah hadn't done his bit—his mundane, smelly, unnoticeable bit—Jerusalem could have fallen, and Israel would have been defeated, and there would have been no kingdom, no Jesus, and no gospel. Yet until just now, you had never heard of him.

I was always inclined to think that God's purposes came about through great leaders, unreasonable men taming the world and defying the odds. Traveling preachers, justice campaigners, people like that. Mostly, however, they don't. They come about through millions of unnamed people doing unheard-of things, in unnoticeable ways, to the glory of God. Repairing a wall. Teaching a classroom of seven-year-olds. Sweeping a street. Running a business. Raising autistic children. Fixing a dung gate.

That, for most of us, should be hugely encouraging. In God's global mission, the role of extraordinary people doing exceptional things is probably far smaller than we imagine—and the role of ordinary people doing everyday things is certainly far greater than we imagine. If you think you're exceptional, that will come as a nasty shock. But when you get mugged by life and find out just how ordinary you are, it's thoroughly liberating. Carl Trueman was right: "My special destiny as a believer is to be part of the church; and it is the church that is the big player in God's wider plan, not me."

The Special-Needs Beatitudes (What Jesus Might Have Said)

Rachel

Jesus talked a lot about an upside-down kingdom. The weak would become strong, and the mighty would be brought down; the humble would be exalted and the proud humbled; the poor would be blessed and the rich undone; the first would be last, and the last would be first. Much of this way of thinking is captured in the beatitudes in Matthew 5. I was thinking and praying about this one day, and I started writing down some special-needs beatitudes on our whiteboard. These aren't in the Bible, obviously, but they reflect what I think Jesus might say about children (or adults) with additional needs:

> Blessed are the autistic, for theirs is the kingdom of
>   heaven.
> Blessed are the tube-fed, for they will be comforted.
> Blessed are the nonverbal, for they shall inherit the earth.
> Blessed are the hyperactive, for they shall be satisfied.

Blessed are the wheelchair-bound, for they shall receive
mercy.

Blessed are those with mental-health issues, for they shall
see God.

Blessed are those in regression, for they shall be called
children of God.

Blessed are those who cannot communicate or understand,
for theirs is the kingdom of heaven.

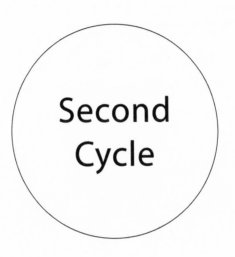

Second
Cycle

Lament

Andrew

Up until I was about thirty, I couldn't fathom why so many of the psalms were about pain. Now I'm thirty-five, and I can't fathom why so many of them are about something else.

Lamenting is a lost art, at least in Britain. In many cultures, when someone dies, those who have experienced loss are expected to process their pain loudly, corporately, articulately, publicly, and perhaps musically: a noisy, guttural, wet, salty lament is widely acknowledged to be the best way to handle the emotion of the moment. In my culture, on the other hand, we weep in private as a family, reflect on happy times, put a good face on things, have measured discussions with funeral directors, tell our friends that we're going to be okay, and then go about arranging a "celebration service" (which must under no circumstances give the impression that anybody is *sad* about anything). Instead of letting the emotion out, we hold it in, push it down, and often find, a few months or even years later, that we haven't really dealt with it at all.

That's why lament is so valuable, and that's why so many psalms in the Scriptures show us how to do it (not to mention Lamentations and Job, which add a huge amount more material). There's something about expressing what we feel in words and music that helps us to come to terms with it and to take it before God in anguished prayer. Christians, in particular, can feel like we ought not to vent our emotions at God; we prefer tidy prayers like "God, we don't understand, but we trust you" to the chaotic, confused, howling prayers we find in the Psalms. But those songs are in the Bible because we are supposed to express ourselves that way. "How long, O Lord? Will you forget us forever? What are you *doing*? Can't you see we're in agony down here, banging our fists against our tear-soaked pillows and eating dust for dinner? If you ever loved us, O God, come and fix things! Now!" If God is big enough to be worth yelling at about your situation, he is big enough to take your pain, hear your lament, and somehow use it to comfort you in the confusion.

And so it was, in November 2012, that I found myself lying on our playroom floor, in the fetal position, sobbing uncontrollably. (I have always had a taste for the theatrical.) For a year, we had been dealing with the fact that Zeke was quite severely autistic and all that this meant: flapping, humming, and repetitive behavior; losing dozens of skills he had gained; going to special school rather than mainstream school. We were coming to grips with the fact that, barring a miracle, he would never take an exam, drive a car, leave home, or get married. The biggest loss had been the death of our dreams, one by one—the myriad of little daydreams you have about being a parent, from sports days to holidays, graduation days to wedding days—but we had consoled ourselves with the thought that we would at least have those things with Anna, even if we wouldn't with Zeke. It was a small comfort at the time, but it was the best we had.

Then we began to notice that something was wrong with Anna

too. Initially, it was a few little things: playing with the sand for longer than normal, performing the same motion repeatedly and being intrigued by it, humming gently to herself as she played outside in the late summer. But as the autumn kicked in, it became clear that things were getting worse, and rapidly. She lost the ability to sing. She lost the ability to form sentences and to string words together. She stopped making eye contact with almost everyone. She got more and more upset about other people being around. One day, she literally woke up and could no longer make star shapes with her hands. Floundering in denial, I refused to believe that it was happening again and insisted to Rachel that Anna was imitating Zeke, rather than experiencing regression herself. And then one day, just after returning from a trip during which I had seen my friend have a very normal Skype conversation with his two-year-old son, I walked into the kitchen, saw Anna flapping and humming—*exactly* like Zeke had done for the past year or so, only (if anything) worse—and it suddenly hit me. I was overwhelmed by the most sweeping, drowning sense of pain and anguish I had ever experienced, ran into the playroom, curled up on the floor, and wailed until I thought there was nothing left. It was, and still is, the lowest point of my entire life.

Lament is more than crying, of course, although it is certainly not less. It also involves putting into words the depth of feeling and sadness we're experiencing: in prayer, in a journal, in a song, or whatever. Doing this forces us to give due weight to our emotions, which many of us (particularly the English among us) are not always very good at; articulating them carefully helps us understand them, as well as handle them wisely. But it also forces us to take our pain to *God*, first and foremost, before we take it to other people. Lament, you see, is about bringing your sorrows to God, in painful description, petition, and confusion, and throwing all your doubts and questions at him. Rushing to dump them on friends, on family, or on Facebook, without having gone to God with them first, is not lamenting but venting, and in the long run it doesn't do nearly so much good. With the best will in the world, people aren't big enough to absorb your grief. God is.

Not all of us will find this easy. In fact, very few of us will. Writing poems about sadness or songs that never leave the key of D minor feels unnatural to most of us, since the society we live in spends most of its time avoiding pain at all costs and is emotionally unprepared to cope with the waves of grief that sometimes crash across our lives. It will feel tempting to jump to the chorus or to launch straight into a don't-worry-be-happy routine, but it is important to give the sorrow a voice, even when it seems strange or self-indulgent. If you're stuck for ideas, read Lamentations.

As someone who has done his fair share of crying and lamenting over the last couple of years, let me conclude with a couple of encouragements. The first is, lament does help. Whether you're wired like me, whereby hysterical crying brings an emotional release that quickly makes you feel much better, or wired like Rachel, whereby you deal with sadness in a slower and more drawn-out way, lament—crying, writing, praying, or singing it— helps you handle it. And the second is, it gets easier. I have never experienced depths like those I felt in November 2012, and perhaps I never will; all the familiar clichés about time healing and grief passing do seem through experience to be true. So if you're mired in despair at the moment, wondering how you're going to get through the week, let alone the year, it's worth bearing in mind that, in all probability, it won't always be like this. The old dreams die, but new ones form. The clouds close in, but the sun finds a way, eventually, of breaking through.

Fighting for Joy

Andrew

Of the one hundred million sentences I have read or heard in my life, the one that has probably impacted me the most is from George Müller's diary: "The first great and primary business to which I ought to attend every day," he wrote in May 1841, "was to have my soul happy in the Lord."[9] In a world stuffed full of priorities, what is the thing that should actually come first? Well, Müller says, my first job every morning is to get happy in God, because until I am, I am no use to anyone.

When you have young children with special needs—or just young children in general—Müller's advice becomes both much more difficult and much more important. It's much more difficult, because you have no control over what time you wake up each day (this morning it was 4:02), and that means you're trying to quiet down an excitable child before you've realized what day it is, let alone had time to pray or read the Bible. Yet it's also much more important, because the risk of muddling through the day, grumpy and bitter, is so much greater. So even if I have to do a few other things first—putting a child on the toilet, creeping about the house in the dark, making a bowl of cereal for him, and saying "Shhhh!" an awful lot—I need to get happy in God as soon as possible. Put differently, I need to fight for my own joy.

For years, I didn't do that. I didn't realize I was allowed to, let alone supposed to. I had never noticed that the Psalms urged people to delight themselves in the Lord and said that the happiest place imaginable was in God's presence. I had missed the fact that the new age that the prophets talked about was one in which people ate and laughed and drank wine in their gardens, and that Jesus got his earthly ministry started by getting a party started and ended it with a barbecue on the beach. I had somehow managed to read the New Testament without registering that joy was one of the most common results of being filled with the Holy Spirit in Luke and Acts, or noticing commands like "Rejoice in the Lord always" (Phil. 4:4) or the description of Christianity as "joy unspeakable and full of glory" (1 Peter 1:8 KJV). To be honest, I had pretty much screened out all biblical passages that talked about being happy, and in doing so, I had managed to collapse joy unspeakable into duty uncomfortable. And of course, I had never read the Westminster Confession (let alone George Müller or C. S. Lewis or John Piper), which said that the main purpose of a human being was to bring glory to God and be happy in him forever. The idea that the Christian life might be about pursuing happiness in God had never occurred to me.

That's tragic. It's tragic because the Scriptures keep telling us to, and showing us how to, rejoice in God. And it's tragic because there are four excellent reasons to pursue joy with all our hearts— which, for the record, is basically the same thing as pursuing happiness. *Joy* is not a stony-faced resilience that sits buried beneath a miserable exterior, in contrast to *happiness*, which involves smiling a lot. As my friend Martin puts it, we are looking for a joy that reaches the face.

The first reason is that the best way of glorifying someone is to enjoy him or her. I glorify Rachel by delighting in her, and we glorify God by delighting in him. The second reason is that pursuing our highest joy in God is how we entered the kingdom in the first place. "The kingdom of heaven is like treasure hidden in a field," said Jesus, "which a man found and covered up. Then *in his joy* he goes and sells all that he has and buys that field" (Matt. 13:44). The third is that pursuing our highest joy in God is also how we fight against sin in this life. The Scottish preacher Thomas Chalmers called this "the expulsive power of a new affection."[10] The heart will always look to rejoice in something beyond itself, so rather than trying to squash desire, we should instead look to satisfy it, specifically in God. And the fourth is that it's what Jesus did, right to the cross and out the other side. "For the joy that was set before him," says Hebrews 12:2, "[he] endured the cross, despising the shame, and is seated at the right hand of the throne of God."

So fighting for our joy is important. C. S. Lewis was right: "It is a Christian duty for everyone to be as happy as he can."[11] The question, of course, is, how? In a noisy, repetitive, tiring household, where is the joy fuel to be found? Various places, it turns out.

Joy comes from the Bible. This is a no-brainer in some ways, but I'm mentioning it anyway because the Bible is the greatest, richest, deepest source of joy fuel there is. I don't read Scripture in the morning primarily to study it academically or to get through my reading plan; I read it in search of joy, like a forty-niner looking for gold—even if I have only a few minutes while Zeke is watching TV at some ridiculous hour of the morning.

Joy comes from other people. If you have disabilities in your household, you may need to think carefully about which people increase your happiness in God and seek them out. You probably already know who they are: people who, when you've finished being with them, make you more joyful in who God is and what he's done. Call them. Get time with them. And pass the effect on to others.

Joy comes from celebrating. This sounds upside down to many of us: we assume that celebrating comes as a result of joy. But in biblical terms, it's the right way up. Think about how the Psalms exhort people to praise: Shout, sing, dance! Bow, kneel! Praise him on the cymbals! Wake up, O my soul! Physically expressing yourself in worship to God—dancing, kneeling, clapping, shouting, singing—fosters delight in God. When all is noisy around you, this can be a great option.

Joy comes from speaking positively. D. Martyn Lloyd-Jones once asked, "Have you ever noticed that most of your unhappiness in life is due to the fact that you are listening to yourself instead of talking to yourself?"[12] That's profound. Actively speaking positively to your own soul—"Why are you cast down, O my soul? . . . Hope in God" (Ps. 42:5)—does wonders. Speaking positively to others doesn't hurt either.

Joy comes from good habits. I remember Pete Greig saying something like this ten years ago: you need to find out what helps you engage with God and make it a discipline. I get happy in God intellectually, so I try to find time with a Bible, a notebook, a hot cup of coffee, and (if possible) a view. There are a bunch of resources—books, chapters, YouTube videos, songs, websites—that I turn to for "emergency joy fuel" when things are particularly challenging. I also encounter God in creation, and since we live two hundred yards from the sea, heading down there in the morning with the dog and looking at the sunrise is a worshipful experience. (Obviously, this won't be possible for everyone, but asking ourselves that question—What helps me get happy in God, and how can I make it a regular part of my life?—is really important.)

Some, if not most, of those may not work for you. That's fine; Rachel's list at the end of this section may help you. But however we go about it, we need to fight for our joy. My first job every morning is to get happy in God, because until I am, I am no use to anyone.

The Quest for Rest

Andrew

With autism, as in life, there are one-off challenges and there are day-to-day challenges.

The one-off challenges are the ones you remember: diagnosis, seizures, hospital admissions, unusually spectacular meltdowns, and so on. Something especially bad happens, you hit a new low, and you cry out for help from your friends and family, who rally around to help in a short, intense, and irreplaceable way.

But it is the day-to-day challenges that you don't remember, which are thoroughly unremarkable and which require no special mention, that are undoubtedly the hardest—the daily grind of early mornings, dressing your children, repeating instructions more times than you can count, trying to remain calm as they insist on buckling their own seatbelt and take ten frustrating and tearful minutes to do it, collapsing in an exhausted heap at the end of the day. Crises are horrible, but they don't last. Normality, meanwhile, rumbles on.

In our case, the most draining day-to-day reality is the lack of sleep. When people ask how they can pray for us or what would make life easier for us, sleep is almost always the thing we talk about first. Rachel has always found it hard to get to sleep before midnight, even when we go to bed at half past nine. And Zeke has now been getting up somewhere between 3:30 and 5:30 a.m. for eighteen months—and when he's up, he's up, and needs constant supervision. The result is that, just as most of our friends are finding that their several-years-long fight for sleep is coming to an end, we're finding that ours is just beginning. From the conversations we've had with other parents of autistic kids, it seems that we're not the only ones with this problem.

So as mundane as it sounds, here are three things we are learning about sleep.

First, we're learning how important it is. John Stott was once asked what the secret of his Christian life was, and he replied, "Knowing how much sleep I need, and getting it." It's a very unspiritual-sounding answer, but it contains a huge amount of wisdom. When you're tired, everything in your life is affected: your physical health, your emotional well-being, your ability to process things mentally, and (because it is often the easiest thing to neglect) your spiritual growth. So it's no coincidence that the Scriptures talk about fasting from various physical joys at times—food, drink, sex—but never from sleep. Soldiering on in exhaustion, proudly wearing the badge of tiredness, can feel heroic and strangely rewarding. But it's extremely foolish.

In our case, this has meant reconfiguring our entire lives to get more rest. Obviously, we go to bed much earlier than we used to. This in turn means that our social life has to be restricted, because we cannot stay up past 9:30 p.m.; it would not be exaggerating to say that we have fewer friendships and spend less time with the friends we do have than would be the case if our children slept until 6:00 a.m. It also means that our involvement in church life and other activities that take place in the evenings is fairly low.

We have someone living with us, and he gets up with Zeke one morning every week. I travel for work far less than I used to. Rachel's parents take the children on Sunday afternoons so we can sleep. Even with all these changes, we're still tired an awful lot of the time. To be honest, sometimes it feels like the quest for rest is taking over our lives. But then we remember John Stott's secret. *Knowing how much sleep we need, and getting it.*

Second, we're learning how to pray and how to process our disappointment with God. It might sound ridiculous to say this, in light of all that has happened over the past few years, but I think the greatest single challenge to my prayer life has been the fact that so many prayers for sleep have gone unanswered. For night after night, I have put Zeke in bed, knelt down next to him, and said, "Father, we pray that you would give Zeke a good night's sleep. Please give him peace and rest, and may he wake up after five o'clock, or even after six. It would be so much better for him and so much better for us, and it would cost you nothing. Please, Father. Amen." Then, the next morning, as the familiar patter of feet comes down the corridor toward our bedroom, I have rolled over to look at the alarm clock and seen in despair that it says 4:27, or 3:52, or 4:41. And immediately the thought comes: *No, God hasn't answered my prayer. Again.*

The strange thing is, over the past few years we have seen dozens of answers to prayer. Yet this one thing, for which we pray more than any other, and which (as it seems to us) has no downside—I mean, seriously, what harm could it do anybody if Zeke were to sleep another two hours per night?—so often goes unanswered. Why? What is the Father doing?

The answer is obvious, and none of us likes it: *we don't know.* It might be to slow us down. It might be to humble us. It might be to force upon us any number of the changes we've mentioned. It might be to give us two hours alone with Zeke each day that we wouldn't otherwise have. It might be to drive us to pray. It might be something completely different. We simply don't know. In all probability, we never will. We've talked a bit about what this means for prayer and handling disappointment elsewhere in this book. But it's probably fair to say that sleep, more than anything else, has forced us to wrestle with these questions and fight our way through to some ways of answering them.

And third, we're learning the importance of perspective. In Julia Donaldson and Axel Scheffler's *A Squash and a Squeeze*,[13] which both Zeke and Anna have really enjoyed, a cantankerous old woman complains that her house isn't big enough, until a wise old man advises her to move all her animals indoors: the hen, the goat, the pig, and finally the cow. Then, when she is tearing her hair out with the lack of space, he tells her to take them all out again. Her house, which she had seen as a poky little shoebox, now seems enormous, and she is overwhelmed with gratitude to the wise old man (even though all he's done is to make her situation worse for a while and then make it normal again).

The moral of the story, of course, is that a change in perspective is powerful. When I roll over in bed and my alarm clock says 4:21, I can grumble that it doesn't say 5:21, or I can rejoice that it doesn't say 3:21. In our case, because Zeke went through an excruciating phase of waking up before 4:00, this isn't even a hypothetical example; on numerous days we, quite literally, give thanks straightaway that he didn't wake even earlier. (We also have a number of friends whose children wake at 2:00 a.m. or so, which adds another layer of perspective.) So for all the aggravation and confusion and exhaustion that we have experienced through early waking—and we know a number of families who have it significantly worse than we do—we have certainly learned a fair bit about perspective. Every morning presents a choice between grumbling and gratitude.

And one day, of course, we won't be tired, and we will enter into everlasting rest. Just not yet.

Children as a Blessing

Rachel

They say that everyone in this world is either a radiator or a drain, and I think there's something to that. We all know those people who energize us, inspire us, and leave us with the feeling that we can do this—and we all know the people who suck the very life-blood from our faith, leaving us tired and negative.

But here's the thing: in a very real sense, kids are always both. Having children, in some ways, is the most irrational decision a person can make. If you want your looks, your bank balance, your energy levels, and your career prospects to take a turn for the worse, you need look no further than having children. Yet at the same time, it is incredible how strong our inbuilt desire is to raise these little people and how intangibly yet lastingly reward-ing they are.

That inbuilt desire comes from a God who is passionate about replicating his image and his family over and over and over again. Genesis is the story of God taking one of the most dysfunctional extended families in history—a bunch of difficult, catty, disloyal siblings and squabblers and scoundrels—and following through on his promise to bless the whole earth through them. And you and I worship God today because through that family then and through millions of families since, he has overridden human failures with divine faithfulness. For God, as for us, children are hugely troubling and hugely expensive. But they are still worth it.

Keeping that in mind is important, because there are very real ways in which children with special needs are far more draining than other children, both personally (to their caregivers) and financially (to the state). We are hugely grateful to live in a nation with a welfare state, one that has poured literally tens of thousands of pounds into the health care, education, and therapy of our children already, and will pour in many times that over the coming years. When our kids were diagnosed, we were told that for the rest of their lives, they would require a high level of support and would most likely never lead fully independent lives. Obviously, we are praying that they confound those expectations, but we know that, at least when analyzed on a financial spreadsheet, they will certainly take more out than they put in. That could both induce a fair bit of guilt (in us) and make our family look like one big drain (to others).

God's great spreadsheet looks quite different though.

This hit me one day as I was lying in Anna's bed, trying to get her off to sleep, and staring at her ceiling. The previous owners of our house had left dozens of little glow-in-the-dark stars up there, and when the lights go out, they sparkle. As I was staring at them, hearing Anna's breathing gradually slow down as she drifted off to sleep, my mind went back to the promise God made to Abraham: your seed will be as numerous as the stars in the sky; in your seed, all the nations on earth will be blessed (Gen. 12:3; 15:5). And it occurred to me that just as God has kept his promise to make Abraham's offspring numerous like stars—there are somewhere around two billion of us on the planet right now, and the number keeps rising—so he will keep his promise to use us, all of us, to bless the nations. "If you are Christ's," Paul says in Galatians 3:29, "then you are Abraham's offspring, heirs according to promise." That means that I, and my children, are going to bless the world. They're not going to be drains but fountains. Abraham's God has promised it.

Practically, I'm not always sure what that means, but I can make a few guesses. Most clearly, our children are a blessing to us, in uncountable ways that I hope shine through this book. Our children have already carried blessings to their nursery one-to-ones, their teachers, their caregivers, and our church community. The naive innocence with which Zeke accosts random people on the street—often, in an uncanny display of upside-down thinking, the sorts of people whom most of us avoid—brings smiles in unexpected places and a welcome to those who rarely get it. A smile from Anna is worth dozens from other children, mainly because it requires so much more work, and her swimming teachers get an unrivaled sense of accomplishment from her little steps of progress. Because our children are secure and tactile little people, they express affection easily and thereby radiate something of the acceptance of God. And simply by being autistic, they draw mercy and compassion from those around them, which increases the currency of God's qualities in general circulation today. Children are a blessing.

Sometimes the impact of special-needs children will be wider reaching. Our friends Steve and Ann have a boy with Down's syndrome, and when he was a baby, someone prophesied over him that he would touch nations. At the time, it seemed like a ridiculous statement, since international travel would likely be impossible for him—indeed for them. Through an encounter with a Kenyan visitor, however, he ended up affecting the Kenyan government's response to learning difficulties: the visitor in question was simply astonished that it was possible for a child in his condition to have such a clear and vibrant relationship with God, and consequently decided to accept a position in a government advisory group on the issue. Obviously, not everyone has an experience like this. But children are always a blessing.

And if that claim makes you want to doubt God's promise, or even laugh in scorn, then bear in mind that the first people who heard it thought exactly the same thing. He questioned it, she laughed, and they called their son Isaac ("laughter") for good measure. Fast-forward four thousand years, and the promise still holds, the blessing continues, and God has the last laugh. He always does.

Joy Fuel

Rachel

A couple of chapters back, Andrew explained why Christians should make joy in God a priority and a discipline. But it's not always that easy. Parenting children with special needs can be like parenting with a mind under siege: the day itself may be silent as you look after a nonverbal child, but you can pretty much guarantee that your mind is not. Sometimes the verbal repetition of the day can send your head into a spin, as your own repetitive worries take over. Some days, simply retaining your own mental health can seem like a challenge, let alone fighting for joy. Here are some of the things that have helped me fight on a daily basis.

Having a healthy distrust of my first thoughts. This may sound strange, but I am learning not to put too much weight in the first thoughts that pop into my head on any given issue. My mind is like a wayward shopping cart: it needs to be continually brought back into line or else it will wipe out some freestanding display. If I don't run my thoughts through some sort of God filter, they tend to go round and round in circles and often lead me to wallow in self-pity in a spectacularly unhelpful way.

Reading a psalm. The Psalms are wonderful, because they remind you that you are not the first person to reach the end of your tether. Often they give voice to what you have been thinking; even when they don't, they help. In a similar way, reading good Christian books—particularly books with short, digestible sections that can be read in bursts—can really feed my soul.

Listening to helpful Christian content wherever possible. Whether it's in the car, in the kitchen, or on a walk, I've found that strong worship music and good sermons can help stuff my head full of whatever is true, right, noble, pure, excellent, and praiseworthy (see Phil. 4:8). You could call this brainwashing, of course—but then, I think my brain needs a pretty good wash.

Remembering the past goodness of God. In Psalm 42, David is not experiencing current joys in God. So he goes back and recounts his *past* experiences of God: "My soul is cast down within me; therefore I remember you" (v. 6). He recalls the past to fuel joy in the present and point him forward to the future. Naming the past faithfulness, provision, and experience of God helps remind us of his track record. Doing that, on some days, has helped me hang on in the mist of confusion.

Keeping a record of the children's progress. Similarly, I find it so helpful to keep a record of where we've come with the children and what battles have already been won. Write things down. Photograph them. Stick them in scrapbooks. Carve them into the walls of your cave, if need be! Human beings are meant to move forward, and one of the biggest joy killers is the idea that we are really just moving in circles. But even if your child is static or regressing, moments of encouragement, if recorded, will feed you on days when it feels like hope is lost and will help fight the lie that you're exactly where you were. (Photos of happy times are also a great help to the children; they remind them of good times and calm them down, so everybody wins.) So record them. On gloomy days, you'll be glad you did.

Learning to play attachment tennis. I recently met someone who does training on how attachment works, and she described bonding with your child as a game of tennis. Sometimes, the parent serves the ball into a part of the court where the child is not standing, and it misses him or her completely. (I try to get Anna to paint or make a cake, for instance.) The child then attempts to serve to the parent, but the ball falls short and hits the net. (She wants me to sing a song from *The Lion King* fifteen times in a row, and I don't.) The game has no momentum, no back and forth, and becomes frustrating for both players. What is needed is for me, as the parent, to adapt my game to the one my child wants to play, however simple that is. So return the serve, stack Tupperware, read the same book back to back, hug them as they watch *Peppa Pig* for the millionth time. For them, that's the joy of the game.

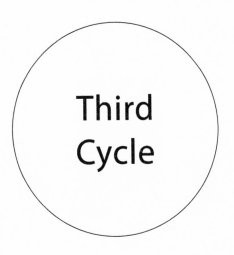

Third
Cycle

The Unresolved *Why?*

Andrew

When tragedy strikes, almost everyone who believes in God, along with almost everyone who claims they don't, asks the same question: Why does God allow suffering? We want an explanation or an excuse—or at least an attempt at one. But very few of us are prepared for the answer that the Bible, Christians throughout history, and Jesus himself seem to point us toward: *we just don't know*. That leaves us in a spin.

Many of us rush in to fill the void, compensating for heaven's silence by providing answers of our own. It's because God gave man free will. It's because a massive miracle is coming that will undo all this tragedy. It's because I did something wrong. It's because my parents did something wrong. It's an attack from the Devil. It's because God wants to teach me something. Admittedly, in any given case of suffering, some of those things may be true (although it's usually hard to identify causes when we're in the thick of it). But even if they are—and often they aren't—we are generally better off acknowledging mystery than insisting upon clarity. An unresolved question is better than a wrong answer.

Right down to my boots, I know that none of these answers can account for all suffering. People don't get cancer or have miscarriages because of their free will. People aren't given Down's syndrome because they're going to get healed later. The fact that our kids are autistic isn't our fault or our parents' fault. People who die in mass genocide are not killed because God is trying to teach them something. So as much as I want an answer, both to the general, global questions and the specific, personal ones, I'm still left with a resounding *we don't know*. The unresolved *why?* is frustrating and often painful, but it does reflect reality.

Fortunately, I know I'm not the first person to find this lack of answers difficult. For starters, I have the Bible, which is full of *whys?* and *how longs?*, including a book-length one (Job) and a particularly famous one from Jesus himself (Matt. 27:46). I also have the wisdom of Christians past and present to draw on and sustain me in my confusion: pastors who have lost their children, hymn writers who struggle daily with depression, novelists who state the problem of evil more powerfully than any atheist could. Though none of them claims to provide a complete answer, they do help us cope with the lack of one.

Here are three insights from Christian writers that, more than any others, have helped me cope with the unanswered questions.

The first is a fairly intellectual one. Most cultures and societies have suffered far more than ours and yet have not seen it as a reason to doubt the existence of God. Why? Because they assume that, if there is an answer to the *why?* question, we wouldn't necessarily know what it is—our knowledge is just too limited. In our culture, though, we assume that the answer to the *why?* question is something we *would* know, and so we get extremely frustrated when we can't resolve it. Underneath our frustration is an overwhelming sense of self-assurance, the conviction that, if something is out there to be known by anyone, it will certainly be known by *me*. Which obviously doesn't follow.

If I go into our conservatory and I can't see Xindel, our giant-sized golden retriever, I can be virtually certain that he isn't there. He's so large that if he *was* there, I would be able to see him. But if I go into our conservatory and I can't see an amoeba, that doesn't really tell me much. There might be one in there; there might be many; there might be none. The fact that I can't see one doesn't mean that there isn't one there. (It's like the tweet I saw the other day from Bill Murray: there is literally no way of knowing how many chameleons are in your house.) In the same way, the fact that I don't know why suffering exists doesn't really tell me much about whether there's a reason for it. If God knows everything, and I don't, the chances are that the reason for suffering might be more like an amoeba than a retriever. So when I start to demand answers, I sometimes think about that, and it takes the pressure off me by reminding me how other-than-me God is.[14]

The second is more emotional and is expressed with agonizing clarity in the great Russian novel *The Brothers Karamazov*. Ivan Karamazov, the middle of three brothers, lists some of the appalling sufferings that strike innocent children—murders, abuse, torture, and so on—and famously remarks that no amount of eternal redemption could possibly be worth the screams of just one tortured child. For Ivan, the problem is not just that the *why?* of suffering goes unanswered; it is that no answer could ever justify the terrible evils that exist.

Yet Ivan also offers another perspective on suffering, which engages with the emotional problem we all face. Humility before God involves acknowledging that although we may not be able to imagine a world where all suffering is made up for, that doesn't mean it couldn't happen; it just means that our minds are limited. In fact, holding to that idea—that all things will one day be renewed in a way that atones for everything bad that has happened, no matter how unimaginable that may be—is at the very center of Christian hope. Paul himself admits that no mind could ever conceive what God has in store (1 Cor. 2:9). Ivan's description of this renewal is beautiful:

> I believe like a child that suffering will be healed and made up for, that all the humiliating absurdity of human contradictions will vanish like a pitiful mirage, . . . that in the world's finale, at the moment of eternal harmony, something so precious will come to pass that it will suffice for all hearts, for the comforting of all resentments, for the atonement of all the crimes of humanity, of all the blood they've shed; that it will make it not only possible to forgive but to justify all that has happened.[15]

In other words, suffering makes no sense now. It isn't supposed to. But in the power and love of God, one day, it will.

The third insight is, I guess, essentially spiritual, and it relates to the kind of God we're talking about. In C. S. Lewis's *The Magician's Nephew*, the main character, a boy called Digory, asks Aslan the Lion to heal his dying mother. Initially, Aslan does nothing. But when Digory pleads with him again, through his tears, he gets a shock:

> Up till then he had been looking at the Lion's great feet and the huge claws on them; now, in despair, he looked up at its face. What he saw surprised him as much as anything in his whole life. For the tawny face was bent down near his own and (wonder of wonders) great shining tears stood in the Lion's eyes. They were such big, bright tears compared with Digory's own that for a moment he felt as if the Lion must really be sorrier about his mother than he was himself.[16]

We worship a crying God—a God who became like us, suffered bereavement and loss, wept at gravesides, and cried out in anguish as he died. So when we experience suffering and face all the unanswered *whys?*, we may never know what the answer is—but we know for sure what the answer *isn't*. It isn't because God doesn't love us. It isn't because God doesn't care. It isn't because he is distant or unsympathetic or cold or merciless. The Lion has tears in his eyes, and although I will never understand all that he's doing, I know that he isn't doing it because he doesn't love me. The cross proves that.

Those three insights may or may not help you, but they've certainly helped me. I don't know why God permits so many bad things to happen, but then I wouldn't expect to—I live in the confident hope that he will one day renew the world, so that even the darkest and most terrible evils of this world will be undone and swallowed up in victory. And I can look at the face of Jesus and remember that, whatever the reason for suffering, it certainly isn't because he doesn't care. Questions still linger, and tears still fall. They probably always will. In the meantime, though, I trust and hope and wait.

Thankfulness in a World of Entitlement

Rachel

If what you think you *have* is greater than what you think you *deserve*, then that's where thankfulness comes from. If what you think you *deserve* is greater than what you think you *have*, then that's where bitterness comes from. Ouch.

That's a challenge in all cultures. In ours, it's a greater challenge than usual, because we live in a world where a good many people make a great deal of money trying to convince us of two things: we deserve a lot, and we don't have enough. (Lawyers and celebrities specialize in the first, advertisers and retailers in the second.) In a particularly ridiculous example of this, I recently watched an ad for a skin-care product in which a husky, very sincere, and supremely confident voice told me that that my skin, my *skin*, had "rights" (to be preserved, protected, moisturized, and goodness knows what else). But as crazy as that is, the thought is everywhere. You have the *right* to a good education for your child. You're *entitled* to benefits. So if you're not getting what you deserve, you either grumble or you fight.

Now, there's a fine line to tread here. We count it an enormous blessing to live in a society with welfare and benefits and special schools and blue badges (parking passes for those with mobility challenges)—especially since we have friends with autistic children in nations that don't have any of these things—and we think it's just good sense to get whatever help is available. I apply for whatever I think might help my children thrive, and that means I've filled out more forms than a Soviet bureaucrat. But as soon as I start thinking of those things as *rights*, which I *deserve* (rather than, say, thinking of them as gifts, since I could easily have been born in Turkmenistan), I open the door in my soul to bitterness, irritation, and frustration. And that kills thankfulness. And when thankfulness dies, so do I.

So I see it as my responsibility to cultivate thankfulness and crush bitterness wherever I can. That's not just a question of personality. It's about theology.

Take my understanding of sin, for instance. If I believe, as I do, that what I deserve is death and permanent separation from God, then every happy moment, sunny day, cuddle with my children, outburst of laughter, or song can be celebrated as a wonderful bonus, which I am in no way entitled to. Or what about my understanding of humankind? If I believe that humans, as we currently stand, are essentially rebels against God who have turned creation into a basket case of sin and wrongdoing, then how much more will I be thankful that, among them, I have found health professionals and caregivers and schoolteachers who (whether they know it or not) reflect their Maker's compassion and care for my children?

More than those things, though, there is my understanding of grace. Grace, by revealing both how much I have and how little I deserve, helps bring me to a place of humility and thankfulness.

I remember enjoying a meal, before we had our children, with some friends whose little boy suffered severe brain damage as a result of a traumatic birth. He had multiple and complex health needs and required round-the-clock care. We asked our friends how they processed what had happened, and they instantly replied that they had been blessed with a child, while many were unable to conceive. For them, like cancer survivor PJ Smyth in the following remarkable quotation, the blessing of a child (no matter what his or her needs) fell well within the I-never-deserved-him-anyway category:

> The greatest enemy to gratitude is a sense of entitlement. The moment you think that you are hard done by and deserve more, then you can wave goodbye to thankfulness. However, circumstances of sickness, death, or disappointment can lend themselves to a sense of entitlement like no other, and so cultivating gratitude and contentment in "all circumstances" can be a stiff challenge in a storm of suffering. . . . I have already received from God way more than I deserve. . . . Anything better than hell is a bonus, a radical bonus of grace from God to me. My eternal salvation, every sunrise, every family member, every friend, every mouthful of food, every article of clothing—it's all fair and square in the I-never-deserved-it-anyway category. . . . Yep, I am a grateful man before, during, and after the storm.[17]

When you start thinking this way, you view child development differently and start to see excuses for thankfulness everywhere. When our children started at a special-needs school, I was struck with what they were able to do rather than what they couldn't do. The fact that we knew what their voices sounded like, that they could walk, run, and climb, that they could swallow, digest, and sit independently, became not *givens* but *gifts*.

Not a single milestone met by our children has been earned

for them by our good living. We're not entitled to any of them. So when milestones do come, we celebrate, crack open the champagne, and give thanks to God, without whose sustaining power neither they nor we would draw another breath.

We've started noticing that every day, even in the hardest ones, God is dropping small but vital gifts in front of us, like those tailor-made presents that float down on little parachutes in *The Hunger Games*:[18] a phone call, a smile, a hug, a person, a financial gift, a meal. Even Charlotte Moore, mother of two severely autistic boys and author of the excellent *George and Sam*, said in a recent interview that only 10 percent of each day was horribly difficult, and an awful lot of the rest was either neutral or positively joyful.[19] By choosing to celebrate how much I have and deciding to remind myself how little I deserve, I can sever the root of bitterness and give thankfulness the soil it needs in order to flourish, both at the same time.

"Give thanks in all circumstances," says Paul in 1 Thessalonians 5:18. Good call.

The Storyteller

Rachel

We all long for stories to end with redemption. That's what drives the stories I love, whether romantic ("I really hope they get together"), heroic ("How on earth are they going to get out of *this*?"), or whatever. Fictional stories, famous stories, everyday-life stories—something in me longs for a happy ending, with all the pain undone and all the suffering redeemed.

When we skip to the end of God's big story, of course, that's exactly what happens. The biblical drama ends with redemption, as the hero defeats the villain, gets the girl, saves the world, and lives happily ever after. But in the meantime, riding the roller coaster through the peaks, troughs, celebrations, and anguishes of parenting, I find it easy to forget who the storyteller is and exactly how that redemption will finally come. I have to remind myself that God is the storyteller, not me. And it is his job to redeem it all, not mine.

That's hard to accept sometimes. When faced with disabilities, particularly those that affect our kids, the temptation is almost overwhelming to create a fantastic redemptive story—one that suddenly, somehow, makes sense of the one in one hundred thousand chromosomal abnormality, or the brain damage brought about by an overworked doctor who arrives late to a difficult birth. We're designed to search for reason in the seemingly senseless events that torpedo our lives, and we want to make sense of them as soon as they happen. So we set up support groups. We volunteer for charities. We raise awareness. We start foundations, we hold fund-raisers, and we cook things and make things and write things. We rush to explain all the ways in which having special-needs children has, despite appearances, enhanced our lives. We strive *daily* to make sense of the senseless, so that the pain we've experienced will not be in vain. In other words, we write our own happy ending.

But we are not the storyteller. We don't have the power to resolve the twisted plot and bring triumph out of tragedy. Only God does. And his timing is often very different from ours.

I would love to be able to come to the microphone at the front of church next Sunday and share a revelation that has come to me of why all this has happened, or a sudden character transformation that has come about in me, equipping me to handle each day in a more godly way. Or best of all, a YouTube clip of my two children making a miraculous improvement as a result of prayer, horse handling, art therapy, or drumming lessons. Then, with my newly communicative kids and my ministry to other parents, I could reflect knowingly on my experience—"Ah, so *that's* why all this happened. What a relief!"—and enjoy my eureka moment. Even in the very act of writing this book, I'm having to resist the constant temptation to think that maybe *this* will make up for autism and that helping others will, in a small way, atone for it.

Of course, there is a sense in which this is partly true. Paul says that it is because of our afflictions that we are able to comfort others who have been afflicted, comforting them with the comfort we ourselves have received from God (2 Cor. 1:3–7), and there is true therapy—and purpose—in that. But we are fooling ourselves if we assume that the benefits we experience will outweigh the losses. For some, they might. For us, at least at the moment, they haven't.

So I have to remember: the story is not mine to save. The pressure to write a story that makes sense of what has happened to us, as acute as it can feel, must be resisted; God is the great storyteller, the divine happy-ending maker, and I'm not. I am a character in God's story, not the author of my own, and it is God's responsibility to redeem all things, to make all things work together for good, and, as Sam Gamgee puts it in *The Lord of the Rings*, to make everything that is sad come untrue.[20] It's only when I find my place in the giant story that God is writing and come to terms with its twists and turns that I can lean back in the knowledge that it is my Father's job to redeem, or make right, all things—not only in our nuclear family but in every single thing that the curse of sin has touched or tarnished.

I may never have a eureka moment in this lifetime. I may never tell a "Nicky Cruz for the special-needs world" story or get linked to on YouTube or have people in support groups use me as an example of how things can turn around. My parenting life may be a continual journey of struggling, learning, praying, crying, laughing, loving, and trusting, with no dramatic resolution and no end in sight. But that's why I cling to the Storyteller, and his unbreakable promise to put the world right. In the end, he redeems it all.

The New Ordinary

Andrew

Human beings are astonishingly adaptable. It's our special genius. We can form communities in deserts and in jungles, up mountains or on virtually barren tundra. We're forever inventing new things and solving old problems, and when circumstances look impossible, we improvise. These days, people can swim without arms, run without shins, and write books by moving only their eyelids, all by using the creativity that comes from being made in the image of God. It's as if we encounter a new difficulty, pause for a while to sort ourselves out, and then think, *Right, we had better get on with it then. This is the new ordinary.*

Put differently, we adapt to it.

For everyone struggling to come to terms with a new or upsetting reality, the fact that we're made that way is fantastic news. You may not feel up to it, and you may not even notice it, but as time goes on, you will adapt to the way things now are. And then one day, you will look around at your life, and suddenly realize that you are unable to imagine what the *old* normal would have looked like. The idea of living the life you once expected, with all that would have involved, will seem strange, distant, or even unimaginable.

So for example, we've gotten used to the fact that when Anna walks into a room, the first thing she will do is remove all the cushions from any chairs or sofas. If she's comfortable with the way the chair looks without cushions, that will suffice; if she isn't, she will remove the part you sit on as well and throw it onto the floor. If your living room has enough seats for several people, which most living rooms do, that might add up to ten or twelve cushions strewn over the floor within seconds of her entering the room—and there's no point in putting them back, because she'll only emit an irritable noise and remove them again. The result is that living rooms with Anna in them tend to look rather like Moroccan restaurants. There may have been a time when that habit was profoundly annoying; I can't remember. Nowadays, though, it's just ordinary. Our family laughs about it, our friends watch with fascination, and we shrug our shoulders, chuckle, and try to coax her into a room without seats.

In the new ordinary, it is entirely unremarkable to look out the kitchen window at 6:50 in the morning, peer down the garden through the gloom, and suddenly notice a semi-naked boy (who you may have thought was still upstairs) jumping exuberantly on the trampoline, squealing with delight, and talking to characters from *Thomas the Tank Engine*. Nor is it strange to have a conversation with at least three levels of reality involved: real people today, real people from twenty years ago as seen on old family videos, and fictional characters from TV shows (as in, "Mummy, can you and Station Officer Steele feed baby Uncle Phil some milk? Please can we do that?"). At the time of writing, it would be thoroughly bizarre, and extremely disorienting, if Zeke were somehow to eat a hot meal. Ordinary has changed, and we've adapted.

The new ordinary involves a lot of hand flapping, humming, and shouting. When the children were first regressing, the very visible symptoms of their autism were almost too painful to watch, both because of their very public (and often embarrassing) nature and because of the future life they represented. Now, though, we hardly notice them, and when we do, we know they mean that the children are excited and don't know how to express themselves or that they are trying to calm themselves down about something. The fact that Zeke bounces all the time and skips instead of walking and accosts complete strangers with a "Hello, man!" used to make me wince. These days, it makes me smile with pride. So Zeke is getting better, month by month. But we are too.

Even their obsessions become completely normal. With Zeke, taking a DVD case with you everywhere is just one of the things you always do, like taking a packed lunch or a coat—to the extent that you really don't understand why other people sometimes stare at him as he shakes the case gently and bobs up and down on his heels. You only remember how strange it is when you interact with another autistic child and find that their obsession is different: opening and shutting doors, or copper piping. (While I was writing this in a coffee shop, a boy with special needs came in, and his noises were such that it was as if a pterodactyl had been released into Starbucks. Then I remembered: Zeke's noises are weird too. It's just that I don't notice them anymore.) After a while, your children's habits, as inconvenient as they often are, simply become part of the music of your lives, and you stop noticing them.

All these observations should be enormously encouraging, especially if you're new to this. God has created us, quite deliberately, with the capacity to adapt to new realities and difficulties in the future, to cope better with the ones we already face in the present, and to heal from the pain in the past. When we first found out that Anna was having seizures, I remember saying, "But we can't, we just can't, cope with an autistic boy and an epileptic girl." Then we found out she was autistic too, and even more so, and it became "But we can't, we just can't, cope with two autistic children, one of whom is epileptic." But I was wrong. God gave us grace, and people helped, and gradually, oh so gradually, we started to adapt too. God willing, so will you.

One Boy and His Dog

Rachel

Children say the funniest things, and autistic children say funny things that other children simply wouldn't say. In Zeke's case, a good many of them seem to refer to Xindel, our faithful and much-maligned golden retriever, who has had to endure not just the standard ear pulling and tail tugging but a fair bit of rough housing (Zeke is currently in a phase of wanting to "fall over the dog") and other eccentric behavior. I recently looked back over my Facebook status updates and made a list of some of my favorites. They might give you a flavor of life in our house:

October 10, 2013:
Zeke just looked at Xindel and said, "O, Uncle Xindel. You are a dog."

October 18, 2013:
Zeke keeps asking to "lie down in Xindel's hair," by which he means to climb over into the boot [i.e., trunk] of the car. It makes me think it might be time to clean out the boot.

April 4, 2014:
Zeke: "O, my sweet Xindel, let me kiss you on the mouth."

July 10, 2014:
Just caught Zeke muttering, "Xindel's just roaming about and defecating everywhere." To be fair, he wasn't, but that's definitely not my phrase he's copying there . . .

August 11, 2014:
Gave Zeke a chocolate bar on our car journey today, which he ate, enjoyed and spread around his face, before letting himself out of his seatbelt and climbing into the boot with Xindel (fairly standard). When he came back, he no longer had a chocolaty face. Trying not to think about that too hard.

December 1, 2014:
Zeke: "Xindel hit me!"
Mum (skeptically): "Really?"
Zeke: "Xindel! Chill-out room! Now!"

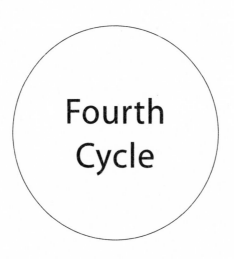

Fourth
Cycle

Handling Grief

Rachel

Grief hits people in different ways. Often it begins a long time before you even get to a doctor's office, whether in niggling suspicions, doubts as you go to sleep, or subtle suggestions from friends and family that all might not be as it should.

For us, going through this for the first time with Zeke, grief took the form of a roller coaster, whereby each day he would present us with contrasting evidence. There were days when all appeared fine and sorted, and those days gave us huge relief. They were often followed by days of awful social anxiety or more skills lost. Then there were those days, too many to count, when we saw conflicting indications in the same day and did our best to suppress the questions and simply wait, holding tight until a diagnosis officially came.

So when we did find ourselves in the doctor's office, there was, to be brutally honest, a peculiar sense of relief that came from hearing our fears confirmed. With that simple sentence, "I think Zeke is severely autistic," we finally realized that we were not awful or overanxious parents and that we could now move on and make the needed changes to our lives. Obviously, the months that followed brought further painful realizations. But overall, it was better to know.

Having been on that roller coaster once before, I assumed that I knew myself a little better by the time it came to Anna's upcoming appointment and therefore that I was more prepared emotionally for what was about to happen. Yet Anna's diagnosis was, and continues to be, gut-wrenchingly painful. Those early days, weeks, and months brought wave after wave of uncontrollable grief. Sometimes I could feel the swell coming, and I could ensure I was on my own in time to process it; sometimes it would catch me by surprise, as I would see a ballet class emptying out of a community center and would immediately have to pull the car over, sobbing.

In the depths of those days, I would retreat to my bed occasionally, and for the first time, I understood what it meant for darkness to cover me and for day to become night around me. Even now, it is Anna's bad days rather than Zeke's that rock me, not just because the severity of her regression is both recent and ongoing but also because, after Zeke's diagnosis, she had represented to us the hope of all the normal experiences every parent anticipates. With Anna, we have had to grieve not just for her but also for the death of many dreams.

For me, it was all so sad that the normal things I would do—like talking to people, praying, reading Romans, worshiping God to a CD in the kitchen—simply didn't work, because my mind was such a fuzzy blur of sadness that concentrating was almost impossible. The two things I was able to do when it was like this, however, were to text people asking them to pray, and to read one psalm. Even now, as waves of grief hit me (as they still do), I usually abandon all other Bible reading and cling to the Psalms, which are so strikingly real, raw, and honest. Psalm 88, for instance, reads, "You have overwhelmed me with all your waves. . . . My eyes are dim with grief. . . . Darkness is my closest friend" (vv. 7, 9, 18 NIV). And so on.

At any rate, grief hits us all, although we all grieve differently from each other and, more strangely, even from ourselves. You may well have heard of the Kübler-Ross model, or the five stages of grief—denial, anger, bargaining, depression, and acceptance—and with both children, I have desperately tried to accelerate my way through the stages and reach the destination of acceptance in a cracking seven days. That, it won't surprise you to hear, hasn't worked. But there were, by the grace of God, three things that particularly helped me in the early days.

One in particular was when my good friend Ann, who is referred to throughout this book for her wisdom and experience, told me about a friend of hers who had gone through the terrible pain of losing her second child to crib death, only six months before Ann's own son Joel was born with Down's syndrome. The friend herself then went on to have her fifth-born child diagnosed with Down's syndrome too a few years later. The friend said, to our astonishment as well as our encouragement, that although losing her baby was intensely painful and tragic, aspects of Ann's experience were equally painful. Her explanation of this was that, with the baby who had died, she did not face the daily grief of milestones unreached, of levels of care, and of fears for the future; she chose to entrust the baby to God. With Ann's son, on the other hand, these things were constantly before her. Clearly, not everyone sees things this way, and for all I know, Ann's friend may have been unique. But it was an enormous help to me. This story, more than any other, allowed me to accept the reality that what had happened to us was very, very sad. And it didn't make me any less of a parent to admit that I was disappointed—not in my child, of course, but in the letting go of good things that I had desperately hoped for.

Something else Ann helped me realize was that one day this will hurt less. Most children with severe special needs will have a preschool diagnosis, which means that you are grieving as you are faced, hour in, hour out, with their meltdowns, seizures, movement problems, or verbal repetition. You are completely submerged in their exhausting needs, as well as trying to hold it together emotionally and spiritually. In the early days, every trip to the park and pick-up from the nursery is an opportunity to be reminded that your children don't do paintings, get invited to parties, or ride scooters. The sheer volume of things to grieve for can seem overwhelming. But as time goes on, these punch-in-the-stomach moments do become less frequent and, in our experience, less potent. That is not to say that we won't find it painful to receive wedding invitations from our children's contemporaries, but at least we will have had time to process the idea somewhat.

Finally, the third helpful insight was the discovery that God can cope with our grief. He is big enough to handle our tears, our disappointments, and all the accompanying anger and rage that go with them. The laments in the Psalms, not to mention the prayers of Gethsemane and Calvary, show us beyond any doubt that God is not scared of our pain, nor does he want us to suppress it in the name of soldiering on. For us, paradoxically, openly grieving before God and before people has been (and continues to be) vital to living a joy-filled life. As it happens, we are now in the lovely position with Zeke of having some of the dreams to which we died, and over which we grieved, being surprisingly brought to life again. (Watching your child learn to sing for the first time is beautiful, but it is nothing compared to watching the child you thought would never sing again launch into the Christian praise song "Blessed Be Your Name.")

But I never regret engaging with the pain of loss, in all its haunting anguish. It makes the victories, when they come, all the more sweet.

Learning to Pray

Andrew

Prayer, for me, can be seriously confusing. I love logical arguments and equations and mysteries that end up with satisfying solutions; I hate unresolved chords and unexplained puzzles and *Lost*. I like dogs: measured, predictable, comprehensible. I hate cats: enigmatic, mysterious, inscrutable. I love clarity; I struggle with mystery. I find reading the Bible easy. I find prayer really, really hard.

There are just so many tricky questions. Is prayer mainly for God's benefit or for mine? Should I pray for the same thing repeatedly until I get it (Luke 18:1–8), or do I pray once and simply believe that I've been given it (Mark 11:24)? Will God always give me what I ask for (John 14:13) or not (2 Cor. 12:8–9)? If God knows what I need before I ask him (Matt. 6:8), then why pray at all? If Jesus and the Holy Spirit are interceding for me (Rom. 8:26–27, 34), then what difference can *my* meager prayers possibly make? And so on, and so on. These questions aren't just theoretical, like wondering how many angels can fit on a pinhead.

I actually need to know as I approach God in prayer, am I seeking to influence my Father here, or am I simply lining myself up with what he's already decided to do? Should I keep pressing on until I get an answer, or does no mean no?

My confusion and frustration boiled over one evening in October as we prayed for the children, and I found myself thumping the sofa in anger that nothing was changing. (There's impassioned prayer and there's irreverent ranting, and you know when you're doing the second rather than the first.) So the next morning, I took our dog, Xindel, to Abbott's Wood, a nearby forest preserve, with the sole aim of praying for the children. The next few hours were among the most significant times of my entire Christian life.

It was a crisp, sunny autumn morning, and I decided to start with the Lord's Prayer before moving on to something else. As it turned out, Xindel and I got lost—I suppose it would be fairer to say that *I* got lost, since he didn't really have much to do with it—and it took me two and a half hours to get from "Our Father" (Matt. 6:9) to "Give us this day our daily bread" (Matt. 6:11). Slowly, as we crunched leaves and meandered through parts of the forest I had never seen before, I talked to God and meandered through parts of the Lord's Prayer I had never seen that way before. God heard me. I heard God.

Our Father. There's something immensely powerful and reassuring, I realized, about starting a prayer with the most intimate form of address there is. Before asking for anything or complaining about anything, I remind myself that the person I'm speaking to loves me, is for me, and wants what is best for me, just as surely as I want what is best for Zeke and Anna. With these simple, touching first two words, I rule out any explanation of unanswered prayer that involves God not listening, God not caring, or God not loving. Everything I say in the rest of my prayer is founded on the truth that God is good, wants to do me good, and will do me good—fathers don't give their kids stones when they need sandwiches (cf. Matt. 7:9)—so if God doesn't immediately give me what I'm asking for, then it's because somehow, ultimately, there is something better. Tim Keller's pithy phrase that "God will only give you what you would have asked for if you knew everything he knows" is a great way of saying this.[21] Just digesting this reality took me a good half hour, by which time Xindel and I were well and truly lost.

In heaven. If addressing God as "Father" highlights my relationship with him, then addressing him as "in heaven" emphasizes his sovereign power, his divine rule over all things, and his totally different perspective from mine. It's a reminder that he can see the whole board and I can't. And I remember being struck by this at exactly the moment when, suddenly emerging from the trees, I found myself unexpectedly in open ground, looking out at a stunning vista that stretched for twenty miles across nonstop autumnal woodland. I had been under the forest canopy for so long that I had lost sight of where I was, but the scope of the view reoriented me in seconds and showed me where to go next. It was one of those moments when creation and Scripture spoke together, showing me that in all my wanderings, I had literally been unable to see the wood for the trees. God is in heaven, and he can see the whole board. I'm on earth, and I can't.

Hallowed be your name. Jesus taught that the first thing to request, before you get on to the way the world is or the things you need, is for God's name to be honored. Praying through this, with my newfound sense of direction, took me to Isaiah 26:8—"Your name and remembrance are the desire of our soul"—and the revelation that, whatever else I care about, God's name comes first. Restating priorities is powerful. And as we reentered the woodland and began our descent, I restated my priority, as defined by Jesus, over and over again: "I don't want to have to choose. But if I do, then God's name is more important than healing Zeke. God's name is more important than healing Anna. God's name is more important than conversations with my children, my career, 'normal' family life, or having grandchildren. Your name and remembrance, O Lord, are the desire of our soul."

Your kingdom come, your will be done, on earth as it is in heaven. Xindel and I had been walking for an hour and a half now, and finally I began to pray for God's rule to be expressed in the lives of our children: in healing, in blessing, in peace, in salvation. We'll talk more about healing in the next chapter, because it's an important topic when it comes to disabilities. But what struck me most, I remember, was that praying for healing and blessing at this point, after spending a while responding to God's love, knowledge, glory, and beauty, meant that my prayers for the children were framed in a right attitude of trust and security, rather than a sofa-thumping anger and frustration. When Jesus said, "Pray like this," he knew what he was doing.

Give us this day our daily bread. Finally, I turned to asking for the more day-to-day needs we had as a family: sleep, health, financial provision, school places. Jesus often talked about bread when he was teaching on prayer, presumably because it represents the most basic of human needs. It's interesting to compare his instructions, actually. Here in the Lord's Prayer, he tells us to pray for the bread we need *today*, as if calling us to a lifestyle of continuous trust. Immediately after this, in the Luke 11 account, he contrasts God with a guy who has to be shamed into providing bread for his friend—the question "Which of you . . . ?" (v. 5) clearly implies that the situation is unthinkable for people, let alone for God. And in Matthew 7:9–11, he points out that since human fathers give bread to their children, our heavenly Father certainly will. By starting with our acknowledgment that God is our Father who is all-powerful and all-knowing and then moving on to ask for stuff, we root our requests in a childlike confidence that, whether we get what we're asking for immediately or have to keep on asking, our Father will give us what is best.

Many of the puzzles of prayer, then, are best addressed by doing just what Jesus said: "When you pray, *pray like this*: Our Father. . . . " Sometimes, as parents, we give Zeke what he's asking for straightaway. Sometimes we give it to him after a period of asking. Sometimes we don't give it to him at all, because we know something he doesn't, and what we have in mind is even better for him than what he's asking for. God, in a far more loving, knowledgeable, and powerful way, works that way with us.

But here's the thing: until Zeke gets what he's after, or finds out what the "even better" thing actually is, he keeps asking. Over and over and over. And so should we—like a widow in need of justice or a blind man in need of sight or an autistic boy in need of *Thomas the Tank Engine*. When you pray, *pray like this*.

Some Reflections on Healing

Andrew

At some point or other, every Christian with a disability is going to have to figure out how to think about physical healing. In our case, theological reflection on healing has been essential: we help lead a large charismatic church that sees dozens of people physically healed each year; I have talked about God's healing power in at least three of my books; we both speak at conferences and churches where people get physically healed in response to prayer; and yet we also have two children with special needs who have not been healed, as well as many friends for whom that is also true. All this, in a very good way, has forced us to think carefully about the subject.

When it comes to physical healing, the extremes are relatively easy to see. We have the loony prosperity gospel preachers and their shallow messages of permanent health and wealth for everyone who follows Jesus. Then we have the starchy cynics who think that everyone who claims to have experienced divine healing is either lying or delusional. The first group acts as if God always heals today because the kingdom of God is entirely *now*; the second group acts as if God never heals today because the kingdom of God is entirely *not yet*. The biblical picture (to summarize a huge amount of theology in one sentence!) is that it is *both now and not yet*. We should expect both miracles and disappointments, physical healing and physical death, to form part of our experience until Jesus returns.

So far, so good. But even when people agree on those things, there can still be confusion. We have Tigger types, who bounce around insisting that God will always heal us if we just have enough certainty that he will, and we have Eeyore types, who mope around mumbling that disabilities are just part of the way things are and that asking God to heal us is a waste of time. Being a Winnie-the-Pooh type in the middle, believing that God wants to heal but trusting him when he doesn't, can be exhausting. The Tigger types make you feel guilty; the Eeyore types make you feel grumpy. And you're still the one with the disabled child.

So it has helped us to realize that, although we often talk as if there is only one type of divine healing, there are actually four, as far as we can tell. Most people instinctively prefer some to others, but they're all there.

Type 1: A virus enters my body, and my white blood cells are launched into action like a rabid dog, hunting down the perpetrator to kill it. I cut my hand, and immediately a combination of clotting blood cells and replacement skin cells begin the patch-up job. Every second, as my heart beats, tiny bits of mineral and organic material are sent to parts of the body that need it, performing ongoing repairs that will never finish, like painting the Golden Gate bridge hour after hour, year after year. My body is being healed all the time, and it's a result of the grace of the God who created me, searches me, knows me, and loves me that he has designed a body that functions that way. I never want to forget—although I often do—the daily wonder of living in a physical body that heals itself.

Type 2: A young man who was born deaf and is attending a training event with me is immediately healed when someone prays for him in Jesus's name; he promptly calls his fiancée with his (until now deaf) ear to the phone and has a (very excitable) conversation with her. A woman, wheelchair-bound for years, is prayed for in Jesus's name, is immediately healed, gets out of her wheelchair, and months later phones the Benefits Office to stop her disability allowance, whereupon she is told that the system does not allow for miracles, so she will have to keep receiving payments (which leads the *Daily Mail* and the BBC to run an outraged story about it). A young woman whose protein allergy immediately disappears, in response to healing prayer, now has the words "miracle cure" in her official National Health Services file. A Jewish prophet lays his hands on blind eyes and deaf ears, with or without mud and spit, and causes them instantly to see and hear. "Whoever believes in me," he says, "will also do the works that I do; and greater works than these will he do, because I am going to the Father" (John 14:12).

Type 3: I cycle into the middle of a main road, aged eleven, and collide with a VW Beetle, with the result that my tibia and fibula are smashed between the car and the bike, and the windshield wiper makes a four-inch deep stab wound in my side, between my liver and my spleen, right before I land on the asphalt headfirst. An ambulance appears within minutes, and a splint is put on my leg. A surgeon removes the glass from inside my torso and then repairs it, leaving only a scar (which looks like a shark bite and is good for parties). My leg is reset under general anesthetic, which kicks in within seconds of being injected into my arm, and after sixteen weeks I am running around again like a normal eleven-year-old. The materials to build the hospital, the oil that fuels the ambulance and enables me to get there before I die from blood loss, the image of God in the paramedics that makes them give themselves to rescuing people they've never met, the wisdom of the surgeon, the intelligence and skill of the thousands of individuals whose discoveries have made operating rooms and anesthesia possible—all these are gracious gifts of a loving God whose mercy enables healings to take place across the world that would, in any other generation, have been considered quite miraculous. No wonder they call him Yahweh-who-heals-you (Ex. 15:26).

Type 4: A trumpet sounds, and the dead are raised in a flash, in the twinkling of an eye, never to perish again. Physical bodies become incorruptible, spiritual, glorious, powerful; no sickness or affliction will ever befall them again. Cholera and cancer are consigned to the cosmic dumpster for all eternity. Operating rooms, doctors, ambulances, and health secretaries become a thing of the past. Nobody cries, except with joy. Nobody grieves. The sterile smell of the emergency room corridor is no more. The octogenarians, who sit, walnut-faced, under blankets in wheelchairs in hospital reception areas, are given a new life and a new youth that will never again be stolen by the long march of time. Every deaf ear is unblocked, every damaged limb is made whole, every blind eye sees. Autism and Down's syndrome and schizophrenia and Alzheimer's are swallowed up in victory. And "the last enemy to be destroyed is death" (1 Cor. 15:26).

There are three helpful things about viewing it like this. First, we remember that God is healing people all the time. Second, we realize that the question isn't actually *whether* God will heal our children but *when*. And third, we see that praying is about asking God to do now what he will certainly do then: "Your kingdom come, your will be done, on earth as it is in heaven" (Matt. 6:10). It's about staring into the furnace, like the three men in Daniel 3, and saying, "Our God is able to rescue us, O king, and he will. But even if he doesn't, we're still going to trust him" (see vv. 17–18).

So we pray for healing. We believe God can heal our children. And we trust him when he doesn't, knowing that one day he will.

Questions and Answers

Rachel and Andrew

People ask you all sorts of questions when you have children with special needs. So we thought it might be a good idea for our friend Emma to ask us a few things, and then for us to give the best answers we could. Some of them relate to stuff in the book, and some are a bit more general.

Emma: What are the juicy and nutritional bits about having oranges instead of chocolate oranges?

Rachel: Huge amounts have been juicy and nutritional, although we've often realized that only in retrospect. I think having oranges of our own has made us really appreciate other people's orange-flavored situations. When we were planning our family, we had very rigid ideas of what family was and how it should work, and we definitely had the tendency to judge others (and the way they were doing things) too quickly. I think we viewed children as mini–sausage factories where, with certain methods and ingredients, you could ensure certain outcomes. The last few years have been really humbling on that score! We're completely convinced that we do not have it within us and that we really, really need God's daily help. We've also realized that a lot of stuff doesn't matter as much as we thought, which has been quite releasing: it's easy to elevate a child's diet or sleep patterns to almost heaven-and-hell importance, but it turns out that the earth keeps rotating if they only eat toast! Above all this, they are gorgeous, juicy, and hilarious and, when all is said and done, a complete treat.

Emma: What do you guys do for fun in your marriage/family time within the boundaries you have?

Rachel: The children are now at school, and because school holidays mean hordes of people, we find more than ever that going to the woods with the dog works well, and we love that. Swimming is a big hit with them, and one of the big discoveries of last year was that kayaking (in shallow water) works too. We've tended to take out memberships at a small number of familiar, nearby places and keep to those during school breaks. Early on, I found the lack of variation frustrating but have since discovered that missing out on busy indoor playgrounds and whole-class gym parties may not be such great losses after all! For marriage time, we keep our evenings freer than a lot of pastors do, thanks to a very understanding leadership team, and because Andrew works Sundays, he takes Mondays off. That is really paying dividends this year, and we love that time together.

Emma: If Zeke was to publish a book, what would it be called?

Rachel: There would be numerous options, but perhaps he'd go for *The Early Bird Catches the Worm—But Guess Who Catches the Early Bird?*

Emma: How do you think about salvation, eternity, and so on when it comes to Zeke and Anna?

Andrew: There's an instinctive answer and a theological answer to that. Instinctively—and I know this sounds fluffy—my understanding of God's character is such that I'm confident he'll save our children, even if they're unable to understand or articulate the gospel. When people ask me this question, I often say to them that if the children died suddenly, I would have many things to worry about, but I certainly *wouldn't* be worrying about their eternal destiny. I would entrust them to a loving Father, and say with Abraham, "Will not the Judge of all the earth do right?" (Genesis 18:25 NIV).

There's a theological side to this too, though. The reason why humanity is held accountable and judged, according to Romans 1:18–32, is that we knew the truth about God and suppressed it. But those things aren't true of a lot of people with learning disabilities, because they cannot sufficiently understand the world. So I suspect people who cannot understand the gospel, because of their disabilities, are going to receive grace from God anyway. (This is also what John Piper argues in *Let the Nations Be Glad*. And he's not that fluffy.) Having said all that, we try to find ways to communicate the gospel to them anyway!

Emma: Like what? How do you communicate the gospel to an autistic child?

Andrew: You do it on their terms, based on what they're into. Some parents of autistic kids think you simply cannot talk to them about God because they won't grasp the concepts (Charlotte Moore says this in her book *George and Sam*, for instance). But as far as we're concerned, we can just start where they are and then incorporate the gospel. Zeke loves music at the moment, so we play Christian music and worship DVDs, and now he pretends he's singing Matt Redman songs on the guitar. Apps on the iPad are often a favorite, so we use a kids' Bible app and let them explore it for ages (even if it means they keep listening to the story about how Jesus got lost or, in one case, start shouting at strangers, "Find the boy! I will be the only King of the Jews!"). They love repetition, so we do the same prayer routine, even if (like Anna at the moment) they don't understand it. Zeke is motivated by chocolate, so we get him to listen to the Christmas story and then open the advent calendar. Some things are extremely difficult, of course—their struggle to empathize makes "Love your neighbor as yourself" pretty hard to explain!—but we trust that God will use what we're doing. He loves them even more than we do.

Emma: Do you discipline your children? If so, how?

Rachel: Yes—although, to be honest, we often feel like we're whistling in the dark, and we deliberately haven't touched on it much in this book because we need someone else to write that one. In general, though, we're trying to sail between two extremes. At one end, there's expecting them to behave and respond like other children, which is what we did with Zeke when he was little. The parenting books all tell you about perfect consistency, requiring immediate obedience, and clear sanctions, but it turns out that autistic children don't work like that (and we probably made several things worse by insisting on it). But at the other end, there's a myth that gets bandied around a bit that children with disabilities are innocent or that bad behavior is all down to their condition, which we're not convinced of at all (either theologically or in practice!).

Basically, discipline takes very different forms, according to levels of understanding. Anna only needs a firm no at the moment, whereas Zeke pushes boundaries continually (and, rather unhelpfully, likes nothing better than provoking a cross face, a deep voice, and a good lecture). Zeke's ability to empathize—to put himself in someone else's shoes—is extremely limited right now, so in turn, he doesn't seem to experience guilt or shame in anything like the way another child might. In an ideal world, we'd love to appeal to his motives and show him how his behavior affects the people around him, but he's not really there yet. So, long answer, but at the moment, discipline for him revolves around giving him clear choices and consequences, as well as doing a fair bit of ignoring in between. We also try to manage his day quite carefully and squeeze in a crazy amount of physical exercise for him, and we tend to assume not much else will get done when he's off school.

Emma: Do you ever find yourself thinking maybe Zeke's and Anna's ways are rubbing off on you?

Rachel: Yes, yes, yes! I (and the dog) find it extremely troubling to take any route to the sea apart from one. Andrew and I also find ourselves continually sequencing our plans for a Monday in a "*first* and *then*" structure, and last year Andrew gave me a social story for my birthday. So where the autism comes from is a real mystery for us!

Emma: What about the water fights in your kitchen?

Rachel: Yes, we had lots of fun last summer introducing Zeke to the idea of water fights, although it turns out there are all sorts of social rules to water fights that I neglected to pass on. For example, throwing a bucket of water over a fully clothed mum in the kitchen at 6:30 a.m., the day after the water fight, will not be met with fits of giggles.

Emma: What are Zeke and Anna's latest achievements?

Rachel: I think Zeke is most proud of learning to slide down the pole at the park, and we're proud of him for dozens of unexpected achievements this past year. For Anna, settling at school so nicely has been a great milestone, and we love hearing the sound of her voice more too.

Emma: How do you negotiate the wonderful world of appointments?

Rachel: There's an African proverb that says, "It takes a village to raise a child," and I feel like these early years have definitely involved input from more people than I had ever anticipated. We have far fewer appointments now, but in the preschool years, we often had several per week (and I have friends who had far more than we did). My approach, if you can call it that, has tended to be to welcome and pursue as many services as possible, which (particularly since the cuts to public services) has involved a lot of phone calls and chasing people. My aim, where possible, is to be the friendliest parent on a return-call list in the hope that even if the person is having a bad day, they might still call me back. Overall, that has probably paid off. I also find that buying chocolates for medical secretaries at Christmas is a good move! I'm not sure if there is a more stressful place to work at the moment than in therapy services, so just saying "Thank you" a lot is good too. I have even considered producing a T-shirt for health professionals that says, "I'm not your mummy, so please don't call me that."

Emma: One last question: how do you approach the whole issue of government-funded social services?

Rachel: If we think we might be eligible for something, we apply for it and let the government decide. I did a lot of soul-searching about this early on, wondering if we deserved such benefits, comparing myself to friends in other countries (in some of which the government doesn't know what autism *is*, let alone make state provision for it), and so on. But we've come to see benefits—and health services, special-needs schools, and the rest—as gifts from God, which we can respond to with gratitude rather than guilt. We've needed all the ammunition available to fight for a happy family life over the past few years, and social services have really helped us to do this. We're grateful!

The Survival Zone

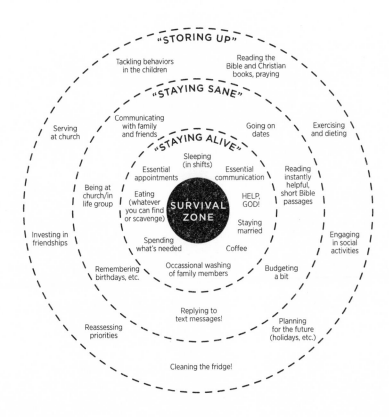

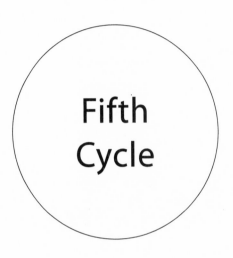

Fifth
Cycle

A Note to Friends and Relatives

Rachel

Perhaps the most profound expression of God's love and grace to us over the past two years has come through the way friends and relatives have responded. A fantastic extended family has helped practically in a myriad of ways. Our group of friends and church network have given countless kind words and prayed faithfully. Our experience of interacting with friends and relatives through our whole journey has been superb.

At the same time, though, we know that this is not always true for everyone. Some reactions, however well-intentioned, can be extremely unhelpful. So since it is hard to know what to say when people are going through a hard time, and since words have such power to build up or tear down, we thought it might be good to give a few suggestions on how to respond when friends or relatives of yours are hit by disabilities, particularly in the case of their children. In saying this, please know that we have gotten this wrong just as much as the next person!

We have found it most helpful when people have simply said,

"That is so hard, and I am so sorry." Many of us find it difficult to stop there; we want to follow up our sympathy with a "But then again . . . " (looking to offset the sadness of the situation), or a "Maybe it's . . . " (looking for an explanation), or worse still, an "At least they won't have *this* problem" (looking for a silver lining). For our part, we would simply say, summon the strength from somewhere, and stop at "I'm so sorry." Particularly within a church context, we can feel the desperate need to put a positive spin on things, even if we call it "finding God in them." Clearly, there is often great value in this—but definitely not in the same sentence, probably not in the same day, and possibly not in the same month. The psalmists do "find God in it." But they give the impression that this is something they fought for, wrestled for, and spent a fair bit of time crying over in the meantime.

Indeed, and this is mainly relevant to parents of autistic children, sometimes the miraculous recovery or breakthrough stories are actually quite painful to hear. I have to be in the right place emotionally to read that article or click on that YouTube link, as they can reinforce the idea that there is a silver-bullet solution out there and that I as a parent am missing it. Some parents and children have wonderful breakthrough moments and understandably want to share them with everyone else. But the reality is that most children with disabilities won't be among the savant few and won't have their whole worlds turned upside down by horse whispering or crochet or the latest therapy fad, and there is, consequently, a very real reason to need to grieve. With Zeke, as it happens, we are currently having some of our dreams for him resurrected, and this is a wonderful blessing. But we are careful to avoid telling other parents how they could copy our methods and emulate our "success." When you have two children with special needs, you realize it simply doesn't work like that.

Practical acts of service are enormously powerful. The apostle James talks about how useless it is to wish someone well without helping them (James 2:15–16), and a good friend of mine told us of how, in her previous church, everyone wanted to pray for healing, but nobody wanted to provide one-on-one care for her child while she attended the church meeting. Our experience, in contrast, has been that people have given all sorts of practical help (unexpected meals left on the doorstep when things have been tough, encouraging cards, free assistance with childcare, even gifts of nights away), and we will always be grateful for that. Acts of kindness that come with no strings attached—no expectation of reciprocity, no desire to be kept in the loop at all times, no roster that needs to be managed—are the best of all.

Finally, I think it needs to be acknowledged that parents aren't the only ones grieving and that grandparents, siblings, extended family, and close friends also have to come to terms with loss. We have really benefited from the speed with which those around us have come to a place of acceptance and the fact that we have not had to justify decisions about schooling, mealtimes, holidays, Christmas, and so on in front of an inquisitorial panel. More than almost anything else, we have really appreciated the leeway we have been given by friends and colleagues to miss birthday celebrations, duck out of evening events, arrive at things late, leave things early, or retreat with children into bedrooms (during parties) and side chapels (during weddings). Yet at the same time, we need to bear in mind that we are not the only ones hurting in the situation, to understand that those closest to us had dreams for our children too, and more practically, to make sure that the needs of our kids do not dominate those of their cousins, friends, or contemporaries.

In other words, for all that friends and relatives have a powerful role to play in helping us, we also have a powerful role to play in helping them. Which is just as it should be.

Faith in Future Grace

Rachel

> Even to your old age I am he,
> > and to gray years I will carry you.
> I have made, and I will bear;
> > I will carry and will save. (Isa. 46:4)

Today is a good day. Both the children are at school this morning, and I'm sitting in the conservatory looking out at autumn colors as I write. Today it's easy to wear glasses of faith as I look at our family's future. But within a day or two, if my track record is anything to go by, I may have exchanged these glasses of faith for my familiar old glasses of fear. Looking through those murky lenses, the future is filled with insurmountable challenges and a never-ending cycle of the same behaviors. Years of wearing the fear glasses have led me to mind games and unanswerable questions: *Well, if it's hard now, imagine what it will be like when they're older, when we don't have our evenings, when they hit puberty. What will life be like then?* At present, I can hardly imagine any prospect more terrifying than Zeke wielding a razor every morning.

It is usually at this point that Andrew, on hearing my concerns, starts ringing an invisible bell and making fun of my melancholic outlook. He calls it the bell of doom and wanders from room to room waving it apocalyptically. You've really got to judge your wife's mood—and your own comic timing—when it comes to this sort of thing, and frankly, I'd say he misses the mark as often as he hits it. But that's incidental.

Seriously, there are lots of legitimate concerns for the future when you're raising kids with special needs. In the UK at the moment, it is almost impossible to plan for care into adulthood, as the whole system is undergoing a huge overhaul, and what will be left at the end is impossible to predict. We all live with often unspoken questions, like *What will the benefits system be in twenty years?* or *Will the children ever leave home?* or even (the question that makes you go quiet over your cornflakes) *What happens when we're gone?* Our children have no siblings to shoulder the responsibility of organizing care, so these questions are all very real.

From my current standpoint, I can see God's grace to me at this point in our journey. Grace, not only as in the gospel but also as in the physical, environmental, common, "every good gift comes from above" sort of grace that blesses and enriches our lives every day. Living in a culture that esteems and values our children. Schooling. Benefits. Housing. Charities that provide equipment and fun days out. A large biological family and a large church family, which both love and encourage us. All these things make our lives full and rich, and they have all been sources of God's provision and grace to us. Every step of the road so far has been covered in grace.

So why is it that even though the scenery behind us has been dotted with beautiful views and oases in the desert, I continue to forecast a land ahead devoid of God's goodness, provision, and blessing? Why is it that though our lives until now have been filled with joy, laughter, and prosperity, I imagine the future as a dark forest in which the occasional cracks of sunlight are outnumbered by worries that we don't even have yet? Why is it that I wake each day and splutter in surprise that God is still being good, and doing good, with all his might? It is as if Jesus were looking at me when he said, in Matthew 6:30, "But if God so clothes the grass of the field, which today is alive and tomorrow is thrown into the oven, will he not much more clothe you, O you of little faith?"

The faith Jesus is talking about here is, in John Piper's helpful phrase, "faith in future grace."[22] For my part, it is very easy to have faith in *past* grace. Jesus did this for me; God provided that for me—simple. My challenge—and (simultaneously) my lifeline—is faith in *future* grace. God *will* provide all my needs. The Father *will* clothe me. The weight of glory that is coming *will* be unimaginably greater than these troubles. I don't know how to share the gospel with an autistic teenager, but the Spirit *will* tell me what to say. Goodness and mercy *will* follow me all the days of my life. The one who didn't spare his own Son *will*, in an even greater way, give me all things.

Faith in future grace means trusting the Giver rather than the gifts. Instead of trusting the benefits we receive (or even the benefits system that makes it possible), we trust the God who has brought them about. Instead of hoping in the help of our families, we hope in the God from whom all families get their name. We have no way of knowing whether our support networks, or even our health, will still be here next year or next decade. All these graces may fade, and every earthly gift will finally perish. But the Giver stands forever, and he will always keep on giving. As time goes on, some of his gifts will come to an end, but they will be replaced by new ones, more suited to our new circumstances and providing more opportunity to trust in future grace.

"Your heavenly Father knows that you need them," said Jesus (Matt. 6:32). And so he does. In fact, he knows what we need before we do. When Abraham needed a sacrifice, he found that the ram was in the thicket already, long before he realized he needed it (Gen. 22:13). That's a remarkable thought. Somewhere, somehow, God is preparing a gift for us that we don't yet need—a person, a payment, a provision, a skill, who knows?—but which will bless us dramatically when it arrives in 2026 or 2041 or whenever it is. Gifts change, but the Giver doesn't. So we can live, daily, by faith in future grace.

gifts change, but the Giver doesn't!

faith in future grace!

Daydreaming about Eternity

Andrew

All Christians, especially those who are suffering, should be daydreaming about eternity on a regular basis. I get that straight from the apostle Paul. "For this light momentary affliction is preparing for us an eternal weight of glory beyond all comparison," he wrote in 2 Corinthians 4:17–18, "as we look not to the things that are seen but to the things that are unseen. For the things that are seen are transient, but the things that are unseen are eternal." Translation: We're supposed to spend our time thinking about eternal things. Dreaming of the new creation. Imagining the world to come.

Mostly poor and suffering people do that, while rich and comfortable people don't. Whenever I travel in poorer parts of the world, I'm struck by how much more focus Christians have on the future in their songs, sermons, conversations, and prayers. In the UK (as in the US), a lot of us have most of the things we want, so we're not in a desperate hurry to have all things made new (except at funerals, when we suddenly start quoting from Revelation). In many countries, however, the brokenness of things is far more keenly felt, and the desire for renewal is stronger. It's interesting, incidentally, that almost all forms of contemporary music—blues, jazz, soul, rock 'n' roll, funk, rock, pop, hip-hop, R & B, and so on—trace their roots to the spirituals sung by suffering African slaves, most of which are Christian songs about a coming eternal age of justice and freedom. When you realize how wrong this world is, it makes you long for the next one.

I'm not comparing myself to an African slave or anything. But I've certainly noticed that the harder things are, the more I wait, hope, and long for them to change. Difficulty, in other words, strengthens my understanding of the future. Suffering produces hope.

I daydream about having ordinary conversations with the children, in a world free of autism, epilepsy, and hyperactivity. In his beautiful description of the resurrection, Paul says that bodies that are currently perishable, dishonorable, and weak will be raised imperishable, in glory and power (1 Cor.15:42–43). That means that Zeke and Anna, in the new creation, will have brains that are able to reason and talk as if autism had never existed. They'll be able to empathize, understand social cues, sit quietly thinking, and imagine what it's like to be somebody else. I daydream about that. I imagine sitting around a dinner table with them, only instead of cajoling them into eating a cracker, I'll be sharing wine with them, talking about why they like it, hearing them make jokes, and asking them about their travel plans.

I daydream about friends of ours and their children. For obvious reasons, a disproportionate number of children we know have special needs. Many of them can't feed themselves, walk, or talk. Yet! But we know how the story ends, as expressed beautifully in "Joy to the World":

No more let sins and sorrows grow,
Nor thorns infest the ground;
He comes to make his blessings flow
Far as the curse is found.[23]

"Far as the curse is found." Like the spring thaw, turning sheets of ice into fresh running water, the power of God will extend to every square inch of this world and turn every curse into a blessing. The tube-fed will enjoy home cooking. The wheelchair-bound will go waterskiing and climb mountains. Those who cannot speak will sing and describe and discuss. There will be no need for words like "syndrome" or "degenerative" and no place for DNA testing, Epilim, Ritalin, hydrotherapy, or physical therapy. "Just as we have borne the image of the man of dust"—fallen, broken Adam—so "we shall also bear the image of the man of heaven" (1 Cor. 15:49). We will have resurrected bodies, just like that of Jesus, bodies that can eat, cook, walk, talk, laugh, barbecue, and socialize, and yet somehow rise indestructible, teleport at will, never grow old, and never decay. O autism, where is your victory? O cerebral palsy, where is your sting?

I daydream about being free from sin. Much of the struggle for me (probably like all Christian parents) is the ongoing reality of, and frustration with, my own sin. It feels so much a part of me that it's hard to imagine life without it, but that is the future I'm heading toward: a day in which I am patient and kind, not selfish, not angry, not envious or arrogant, not irritable or bitter, but in which I believe all things, hope all things, endure all things (see 1 Cor. 13:4–7). One day I will love, forever. One day I will be like Jesus, forever. I'm not sure Rachel will recognize me—but I suspect she'll think that's a trade-off worth making.

I daydream about the new world imagined by Isaiah and Amos and Paul: freedom from futility, with abundance everywhere, the mountains flowing with sweet wine, every house having its own vineyard, and the ground producing crops so fast that the ploughman overtakes the reaper. Perhaps the oceans will turn fresh. Perhaps we'll be able to see all the stars. Perhaps the dead planets outside our solar system will spring into glorious life. Oddly, postapocalyptic movies always depict the world as bleaker, emptier, and grayer than the one we have now, but biblically speaking, it's the opposite way around: the world to come will have a fruitfulness, a palette of color, a sparkle to it that our current world only hints at. It's like what C. S. Lewis says at the end of *The Last Battle*: "The reason why we loved the old Narnia so much is because it sometimes looked a little like this."[24] Further up and further in.

And I daydream about seeing him. For all the excitement of seeing a world in which death has been swallowed up in victory and all that goes with it—exploring, flying, talking to Zeke and Anna in a new way—the centerpiece is always Jesus. Revelation 21 pictures the return of Christ as a wedding, and for all the decorations and flowers, clothes and hats, food and champagne you get at weddings, the bride and the groom are really only interested in each other. On that day, he will be at the center, and all else will fade into the background, like stars eclipsed by the rising sun. Now we see as through a glass darkly; then we shall see face to face. I can only imagine.

Daydreaming about eternity is a great habit to develop while we wait. This light momentary affliction is preparing for us an eternal weight of glory that is beyond all comparison. For what is seen is transient; what is unseen is eternal.

Marriage on Fire

Rachel

In many ways, it is amazing that any marriages survive raising children with special needs. Those that do are a wonderful testimony to the grace of God and certainly not (at least in our case) a wonderful testimony to our resilience and strength of character. A relentless schedule of specialist appointments, filling out forms, meetings, unexpected hospitalization, repetition, persistent sleep deprivation, difficult mealtimes, public embarrassments, and financial pressures can create a lethal cocktail for any marriage. When you add in the personal disappointments and frustrations most parents experience and the sense of disenfranchisement that comes with them, it is not at all surprising to learn that according to a recent Families and Children Study, a higher percentage of single-parent families (vs. two-parent families) in Britain have a child with special needs.[25]

So let's just come out and say it: raising children with special needs is hard on a marriage. When a child has a disability, it is more than likely that one parent will take on the role of caregiver at home, while the other will become the sole breadwinner. Operating in these two very different worlds presents all sorts of marital challenges. The woman (usually) faces the brunt of the day-to-day difficulties, and the man (often) faces the guilt and shame of being unable to protect her from them.

The story I had planned for my life was turned upside down with the birth of our two children. Even as a child, I had been ambitious and driven about achievements at school, and I was sure that an exciting and rewarding career lay ahead. Like most British girls, I suppose, I saw marriage and motherhood as being a chapter of life or maybe a background plot. I married young, went on to get a first-class degree, and was accepted into a competitive internship program.

Like many young women, I was aware that motherhood would be a hefty challenge, and once I discovered I was pregnant, I did what I could to prepare, just as I would for any other great challenge. I read, sought advice from people I respected, prayed, and studied other parents—both those I wanted to imitate and those I was sure I did not! But what I hadn't anticipated was that this was not the sort of challenge you could carb up for in advance. It was hugely demanding but not in the sorts of ways I had expected or experienced previously. There was no structure provided and no feedback available. There was no appraisal system, which meant there was no way of knowing whether you were performing your duties well or badly. Days were monotonous and lacked adult conversation. It felt like being in a workplace where someone had systematically and yet for no apparent reason excluded you from all the meetings and left you on the factory floor on your own.

That much, I imagine, any stay-at-home parent will tell you. But when we first suspected, and then had confirmed, that the children had special needs, it simply added to the isolation and disillusionment that I experienced—and crucially, from a marriage point of view, the gap between Andrew's daily experiences and mine grew wider and wider.

Prior to getting Zeke diagnosed, we were trying to follow the (generally excellent) advice we had come across in parenting guides and manuals but were finding that they simply did not seem to work. I was increasingly aware that our children were different from their peers and that the normal parenting rules did not apply. We would go to toddler groups, and as they ignored the toys and activities and wandered around aimlessly, I would look around wondering, *Why are we here? Why can't they do what the other children can do?* These weekly opportunities to compare the children with their contemporaries brought me to the realization, much earlier than Andrew, that our children were different, so I realized that we needed to treat them differently. Fewer words. More flexible eating requirements. Movable boundaries. Avoiding lecturing them as much as possible (Zeke, quite genuinely, finds a lecture so stimulating that he thinks it is a game and will repeat the behavior in order to get another). And so on.

Andrew, on the other hand, wanted us to persevere down the traditional road of family life: clear boundaries, lots of verbal encouragement, firm discipline, sanctions where necessary. Our parenting became disjointed, causing friction between us. We tried hard not to be controlled by the children and yet to continue to lead in the church, offer hospitality, be generous financially, budget frugally, and work long hours as we had always done. Before entering church work, Andrew had been a management consultant in the city, and he was determined that just because he worked in a church, he would not drift in late and clock out early. But trying to hold to all these principles, in the face of very new circumstances, was taking its toll on me.

Because Andrew was working, I did most of the appointments and hospital stays and check-ups, and as I fed back to him later, describing alien concepts like *sensory needs*, I would get the distinct impression that he was not convinced. My daily routine was about learning and integrating all this new information into parenting; meanwhile, he was concerned that I was being bamboozled by woolly social-care mumbo jumbo and becoming a pushover (which, at times, I probably was). We were pulling in different directions, and the strain was increasing.

At the same time, Andrew was working hard, and even harder at home, hoping each day to come back to a happy family—only to walk through the front door into more tears and shouting. He did the early-morning shifts as my sleep deteriorated, took the children for long drives on Saturdays to give me some space, and spent hours on the trampoline with Zeke when I had lost the emotional energy and motivation to try anymore. I remember how defeated I felt when he first said that his "day off" was by far the most exhausting day of his week. This isn't what I had wanted for him, but I just didn't have the reserves to do anything about it.

In the rainy February of 2013, things came to a head. We had had a particularly difficult few weeks, struggling over what more sacrifices could be made, and things were almost at the breaking point: Anna had been hospitalized again, Andrew had been away for two days, and I had nothing left in the tank. Reluctantly at first, Andrew eventually agreed to cancel all his traveling commitments for a period of six months, decline all future invitations, and start working nine-to-five locally. Gradually, the strain decreased as we identified more with each other's lives and the challenges of care day in, day out. He began to understand the limitations of traditional parenting when it came to our children. I knew that he was in the thick of it with me. Our marriage improved.

It seems so obvious now, but at the time, that small sacrifice seemed like too much. Throughout those early months of recognizing that the children had special needs, we had been desperately clinging to the idea that there must be limits to the control they were able to wield with their meltdowns, refusal to eat, erratic behavior, and sleeplessness. We were trying to live the lives we had always expected, even as life was imploding around us. Two years later, having learned some painful lessons, we have conceded huge amounts of ground on our previous standards for raising children—Zeke only ate toast and cereal for a year, Anna is allowed to lick metal railings, and so on—and we would never go back.

In the end, because we refused to let our marriage go, we had to agree to let a lot of other stuff go. We've gotten to a point where we've decided that our life simply cannot operate like other people's, and certainly not like other leaders'. We've acknowledged that there are some things that *might* help our children, but we simply don't have the capacity to do them, because it would put our relationship under too much strain. I've often wondered, actually, whether having a marriage at the end of it all might be the biggest challenge that special-needs families face. But if we can recognize it for the explosive battle that it is, rather than the peacetime jaunt we hoped it would be, then at least we can throw all our best firepower at the challenges and concede more ground in other areas to protect something that is truly valuable in God's sight.

One final thought: the breakthrough came, when it did, not by me talking to Andrew but by me talking to God, who talked to Andrew. It didn't result from a sustained period of banging the "you need to be home more" drum. It was just one line from the Lord—"Your life for your wife," in this case—and the trajectory of our marriage changed. (Happily enough, nothing rhymes with husband.) I'm sure there's a lesson in there somewhere.

Some Helpful Resources

Rachel

Over the past few years we've found a number of books and other resources helpful because of what they say about either autism, Christianity, parenting, or all three. Here are a few key works:

desiringGod.org. This superb (and massive) website, built around John Piper's preaching and writing ministry, has a substantial number of resources on special needs and disability.

EllenStumbo.com. Ellen has one daughter with Down's syndrome and another with cerebral palsy and an attachment disorder. She writes an excellent blog with resources that encourage special-needs parents, covering a wide range of topics, including adoption. This is probably the best Christian resource on the subject I've found online.

Greig, Pete. *God on Mute: Engaging the Silence of Unanswered Prayer*. Eastbourne, UK: Kingsway, 2007. This book does exactly what it says on the tin: through the story of his wife, who has epilepsy, Pete Greig talks directly and honestly about unanswered prayer, looking at why it happens, what it feels like, and how to live with the silence.

Higashida, Naoki. *The Reason I Jump: One Boy's Voice from the Silence of Autism*. Translated by David Mitchell and Keiko Yoshida. London: Sceptre, 2013. This hugely successful book is written by an autistic Japanese teenager and describes what autism is like from the inside, so to speak. If you're trying to understand what it feels like to have autism, this is the place to turn.

Jankovic, Rachel. *Loving the Little Years: Motherhood in the Trenches*. Moscow, ID: Canon, 2010. Rachel Jankovic has five young children and writes (very well!) about motherhood from a robustly Christian perspective. This is probably the most helpful book on parenting we've read, even though it doesn't talk about special needs at all, because it focuses on where the struggles are really taking place: inside our minds and hearts.

Keller, Timothy. *Walking with God through Pain and Suffering*. New York: Hodder & Stoughton, 2013. This is probably the go-to contemporary book on suffering from a Christian perspective. If you're intellectually wired, or doubting, start at the beginning; if you want resources to help you in your Christian walk, start with the last part and work backward.

Miller, Paul E. *A Praying Life: Connecting with God in a Distracting World*. Colorado Springs: NavPress, 2009. One of the best books on prayer you will find anywhere, *A Praying Life* also engages extensively with special needs through the experience of Paul Miller's daughter, who is autistic. As well as being excellent on its main subject, the book has some wonderful anecdotes, insights, and ideas about raising children with special needs.

Moore, Charlotte. *George and Sam*. Rev. ed. London: Penguin, 2012. Moore is a journalist who has two severely autistic boys, one of whom regressed unusually late, and another boy with no special needs at all. This book tells her story, and although I wouldn't agree with all of it (especially her thoughts on religion), it is both beautifully written and full of insights that make autism comprehensible to those with no experience of it.

Reinke, Tony, and Karalee Reinke, eds. *Mom Enough: The Fearless Mother's Heart and Hope*. Minneapolis: Desiring God, 2014. A super compilation of short chapters from various women—Christina Fox, Gloria Furman, Christine Hoover, Rachel Jankovic, Rachel Pieh Jones, Carolyn McCulley, and Trillia Newbell—this book highlights both the dignity and sacrifice of motherhood in a way that few others do.

Epilogue

THE CAPTAIN

Rachel

Lots of the incidental details in this book are already out of date. The children are always changing, obviously. References to popular culture quickly become obsolete. Future trends in special-needs education and the waxing and waning of the welfare system are thoroughly unpredictable. It can be rather scary.

Even in the time it took us to write this book, for example, the children's rate of development has changed. Zeke has made incredible progress with speech and understanding (which has brought with it some hefty behavioral challenges!), while in the six months following "The Day of Deep Breaths" chapter, Anna regressed for a further six months, leaving her play and development several years behind her brother's. As soon as we get our heads around the children we're dealing with, the rules of the game change all over again. It's probably a common experience.

All of this serves as a crucial reminder: I am not the captain of this ship. I like to believe that I am and act as if I am, but I'm not. We've made dozens of predictions that have turned out, in time, to be spectacularly false—about their development, behavior, habits, education, diets, sleep patterns, discipline, and who knows what else—and they don't seem to be getting any more accurate. We are, at best, sailing desperately into the fog, with ever-changing winds, choppy waters, blank maps, and no real idea what we're doing.

But God is the Captain. He is the navigator, mapmaker, and expert. He sets our course and knows where the land is. In light of that, my continued attempts to reclaim control of the ship are strikingly ridiculous.

I have no idea of the extent to which either or both of the children will reach destinations like independent living. I have absolutely no clue as to how to raise an autistic teenager. I cannot imagine how we will cope with aggression or frustration when the children are older or how we will teach them life skills. The idea of Zeke or Anna becoming adults is virtually unimaginable to me.

Yet what we've tried to convey in this book is that, as uncertain as our voyage is, there are solid landmarks ahead that are knowable and concrete because of the Captain. I know that the future will include the grace, blessing, and goodness of God. I can be confident that he will provide for us and for them. I know he will sustain us all. I know he will journey with us to the very end, at which point everything that is perishable and incomplete will be gloriously resurrected and healed.

So I fix my eyes, not on what is seen but on what is unseen. And I take a deep breath.

Notes

1. Piedro® boots are orthotic shoes designed for children with disabilities or children who require extra arch or ankle support.
2. Horatio Spafford, "It Is Well with My Soul" (1873).
3. William Cowper, "God Moves in a Mysterious Way" (1774).
4. Stimming, or self-stimulatory behavior, is the repetition of physical movements or sounds or the repetitive movement of objects and is prevalent in people with autistic spectrum disorders.
5. Rachel Jankovic, *Fit to Burst: Abundance, Mayhem, and the Joys of Motherhood* (Moscow, ID: Canon, 2013), 17.
6. The *News of the World* was a long-running UK newspaper (est. 1843) that closed its doors in 2011 due to a scandal involving the hacking of phones.
7. Rachel Jankovic, *Loving the Little Years: Motherhood in the Trenches* (Moscow, ID: Canon, 2010), 11.
8. Carl Trueman, "An Unmessianic Sense of Non-Destiny," Reformation21, April 2010, http://www.reformation21.org/articles/an-unmessianic -sense-of-nondestiny.
9. George Müller, *The Diary of George Müller*, compiled by A. J. Rendle Short (London: Pickering & Inglis, 1956), entry for May 7, 1841.
10. The title of a famous sermon by Thomas Chalmers (1780–1847).
11. From a letter to Sheldon Vanauken, in Vanauken's book, *A Severe Mercy* (San Francisco: Harper & Row, 1977), 189.
12. D. Martyn Lloyd-Jones, *Spiritual Depression: Its Causes and Cures* (Grand Rapids, MI: Eerdmans, 1965), 20–21.

13. Julia Donaldson and Axel Scheffler, *A Squash and a Squeeze* (London: Macmillan, 2004).
14. This illustration is adapted from the philosopher Alvin Plantinga, *Warranted Christian Belief* (New York: Oxford University Press, 2000), 466–67.
15. Fyodor Dostoevsky, *The Karamazov Brothers*, trans. Constance Garnett (Ware, UK: Wordsworth, 2007), 257.
16. C. S. Lewis, *The Magician's Nephew* (New York: Scholastic, 1988), 142.
17. PJ Smyth, transcribed from one of his sermons.
18. *The Hunger Games* is a trilogy of adventure novels written by Suzanne Collins, which have also been developed into films.
19. Charlotte Moore, *George and Sam*, rev. ed. (London: Penguin, 2012).
20. J. R .R. Tolkien, *The Lord of the Rings*, part 3, *The Return of the King* (New York: Ballantine, 1966), 246.
21. Tim Keller, Twitter post, April 25, 2013, 8:30 a.m., https://twitter.com /timkellernyc/status/327444450064351233.
22. John Piper, *Future Grace: The Purifying Power of the Promises of God*, rev. ed. (Colorado Springs, CO: Multnomah, 2012), 1.
23. Isaac Watts, "Joy to the World" (1719).
24. C. S. Lewis, *The Last Battle* (New York: Harper Collins, 1956), 216.
25. Natalie Maplethorpe, Jenny Chanfreau, Dan Philo, and Clare Tait, "Families with Children in Britain: Findings from the 2008 Families and Children Study (FACS)," Department for Work and Pensions, Research Report No. 656 (Norwich, UK: Department for Work and Pensions, 2010), 300, accessed June 23, 2015, https://www.gov.uk /government/uploads/system/uploads/attachment_data/file/214426 /rrep656.pdf).

Scripture Index